CONTENTS

MINISTRY OF DEFENCE

Review of the results of investigations carried out by the Ministry of Defence in 1986 into the fate of British servicemen captured in Greece and the Greek Islands between October 1943 and October 1944 and the involvement, if any, of the then Lieutenant Waldheim.

HER MAJESTY'S STATIONERY OFFICE

First published 1989
ISBN 0 11 772664 8

SUMMARY OF THE REPORT

1. Scope of the Review

1.1 This Review was established in the light of the 1988 report of the Austrian Commission of Historians on the wartime service of Kurt Waldheim. Its task was to re-examine the results of the investigation carried out by the Ministry of Defence in 1986 into the fate of fourteen British servicemen, thirteen of them Special Forces personnel, who fell into German hands in Greece and the Greek Islands, and the involvement, if any, of the then Lieutenant (Lt.) Waldheim in their fate.

1.2 In addition to re-examining the much-discussed cases of the parties of Allied servicemen captured off Alimnia, at Yannina and on Calino which were first looked at in 1986, the Review has addressed those additional cases raised since 1986, notably the party captured off Cephalonia.

1.3 It has investigated too the fate of other captured British servicemen who it has been possible to identify personally and who, as members of the Special Forces or the Allied Military Mission, were likely to be considered by the Germans to fall within the category of 'commandos'. Throughout the Review the term 'commando' is used to denote members of the Special Forces and special organisations including the Royal Naval personnel operating the vessels used to transport these forces. The Special Forces concerned were not strictly speaking 'commandos': i.e. members of Army or Royal Marine Commando Units. But as the Germans used the word, it has been adopted as a generic term to distinguish the cases and type of operations to which the Germans applied the terms of a special order defining treatment of prisoners. In contrast with the treatment of prisoners of war from conventional units or those engaged in what the Germans considered to be conventional warfare, an order issued on Hitler's authority on 18 October 1942 said that all Allied troops deemed to be involved in 'so-called "commando" operations' should be exterminated to the last man in combat or in pursuit and that as a general principle no quarter was to be given. This order is referred to throughout this Report as the 'Commando Order'.

1.4 In all, the 'commando' cases identified as such by the Germans and considered here involved thirty British and Commonwealth servicemen. Of these, seven did not survive the war and are believed to have been executed under the 'Commando Order': Capt. Warren of the Cephalonia party, probably executed in late May 1944; Sub/Lt. Tuckey, L/Sgt. Miller, Pte. Evans, Gnr. Jones, Pte. Rice and Telegraphist Carpenter of the Alimnia party. All but the last were probably executed soon after 27 April 1944; while Carpenter was probably executed sometime after 4 June 1944. Of the other twenty-three, all but one survived German imprisonment and either escaped to re-join the Allies or were liberated from prisoner of war camps at the end of the war. The exception was Pte. Fishwick who died soon after being taken prisoner of wounds received in battle before his capture.

1.5 Some cases of 'non-commando' prisoners which have been brought to the attention of the Ministry of Defence have also been examined. In addition a number of similar cases of 'non-commandos' were examined during the team's research.

1.6 From the 'non-commando' cases examined a clear pattern emerges of the treatment of almost all such men as standard prisoners of war. These include the cases of Special Forces personnel engaged in 'commando operations' who the Germans failed to categorise as 'commandos'. Therefore only the cases brought to the attention of the Ministry of Defence where illegal treatment was implied or where it was discovered by the Review team and those of the 'commandos' mentioned earlier in this paragraph have been included in this Report. Of the fifty-four servicemen concerned in these cases, only one (Pte. Turton) was not treated as a prisoner of war proper and is believed to have been executed.

1.7 The additional cases have been examined for several reasons. It was necessary to ascertain whether or not they contained any evidence that Lt. Waldheim was involved in them. The records relating to these men and any investigations concerning them might have contained information directly relevant to the main cases under review. Finally it was considered important to try and establish if there was a pattern in the treatment of such prisoners which would throw light on the events and responsibility in the main cases.

2. Sources

2.1 The Review has made use of a wide range of material. Of especial importance have been the surviving contemporary German military documents held in the Military Division of the Federal German Archives in Freiburg and the microfilm copies of these documents held by the United States National Archives in Washington. This material has been complemented by records in the United Kingdom, both those in the custody of the Public Record Office and others held in Government archives elsewhere. A most important source was the records of the war crimes investigations carried out by the United Kingdom at the end of the war. Documents from other relevant archives have also been consulted.

2.2 The Review has been given access to and assistance from all relevant British official archives including those of the security and the intelligence services. As far as possible, the most important documents from these sources have been reproduced as annexes to the Report. However an exception has had to be made in the case of a small number of official documents from the records of the security and intelligence services (which for reasons of security are unlikely to be opened in the Public Record Office) and from a few files from other departments (which have not been released to the Public Record Office on account of the need to respect confidentiality in relation to individuals). The Review has had full access to these documents and, where it has not been possible to reproduce them either an extract from them or the gist of their contents is given in the text of the Report. Professor Sir Harry Hinsley has also examined them all and attention is drawn to his statement at the beginning of the historical report that

I have studied such documents as cannot be reproduced as annexes either in full or at all, and I am satisfied that when summarising or drawing conclusions from them the authors of the Report have properly represented their contents.

2.3 The recent work of other bodies and individuals on this subject—notably that of the Austrian Commission, the World Jewish Congress and Thames Television—has also been studied and has provided valuable assistance. While allowance has to be made for the passage of time since these occurrences and its effects on the clarity of recollection, considerable use has been made of the oral testimony of survivors of these events from both the Allied and German sides, especially as a means of supplementing and clarifying points in the contemporary records.

3. The allegations

3.1 The main allegations concerning the then Lt. Waldheim and the British servicemen in question were first raised in 1986 and have since been repeated. They are that, as an officer in the Headquarters Staff of Army Group E at Salonika during the year 1944:

a. he was personally involved in the interrogation of, or in the organising and control of matters relating to, a number of British servicemen held as prisoners by the Germans—notably the men captured off the island of Cephalonia, on the island of Alimnia, near Yannina, and on the island of Calino—and, therefore, that he was culpable of any mistreatment of British prisoners which occurred.

b. he was personally involved in the decision and perhaps gave or relayed the orders to transfer British prisoners to the Nazi Party's Sicherheitsdienst (SD) for 'Sonderbehandlung'* under Hitler's 'Commando Order', which in some cases resulted in their execution (as is believed to have been the fate of the Alimnia men and Capt. Warren of the Cephalonia party).

c. in a report on Capt. Warren (the leader of the Cephalonia party) he falsely classified him as a 'saboteur' with the consequence that Capt. Warren was considered to fall into the category of individuals liable for Sonderbehandlung and was executed.

d. as the British servicemen in sub-paragraph a.–c. above were subjected to treatment that violated the laws of war, and because Lt. Waldheim was involved in or responsible for such treatment, he is therefore a War Criminal—being in these cases at least an 'accessory' even if not a 'principal'.

e. he was personally involved in some manner in the illegal shooting of a number of Allied prisoners of war from the Laterina Camp in Italy.

In support of these charges, other claims have been made concerning Lt. Waldheim's role and authority within the Headquarters which suggest that:

* The term, which in effect means 'special treatment', a euphemism for execution, is used throughout the Report in the German form.

f. he was an important and powerful staff officer whose authority far outreached his military rank, whose views and suggestions carried great weight with his superiors even up to the Commander-in-Chief, and who was able to influence their decisions in areas outside his official concern, making him to some extent responsible for the results of such decisions.

g. because of his position within Army Group E's Headquarters, he was of such value as a potential source of intelligence that he was actively sought by the Allies and was placed on an Allied 'Wanted List' during the war.

It has further been asserted that:

h. Lt. Waldheim's wartime role in the Balkans was known to the British authorities; that he had been accurately identified in British records and that as these included evidence of his culpability in relation to war crimes against British personnel, he was noted as a war crimes suspect; and that these matters were known during the war and the immediate post-war years, as well as in 1970 when he first stood for the post of Secretary General of the United Nations.

i. the above mentioned records were deliberately destroyed or concealed to protect Lt. Waldheim because he had been of assistance to British intelligence.

4. Legal Principles

4.1 Consideration of the evidence in the light of the allegations outlined above was guided by the following legal principles established by the International Military Tribunal at Nuremberg and in the subsequent war crimes trials:

a. The 'Commando Order' was unlawful.

b. The handing over to the SD in accordance with the 'Commando Order' of prisoners of war with the result that they were killed was a war crime.

c. A staff officer is not a war criminal by reason only of his knowledge of illegal acts, nor can he be held responsible for the outcome of his commander's orders which he approves from the point of view of form and issues on his commander's behalf. He must be the one who orders, abets or takes a consenting part in the crime.

4.2 The issue that had to be examined, therefore, was whether there was evidence that Lt. Waldheim not only knew about the Order but was involved in its execution to an extent which met the normal requirements for prosecution.

5. Conclusions regarding Lt. Waldheim's general involvement: his position and duties at Army Group E Headquarters

5.1 In order to assess Lt. Waldheim's possible involvement in war crimes, the Report has examined his position and duties within the Headquarters of Army Group E in the context of the general command structure of the German Armed Forces and, more specifically, of the operations and organisation within the relevant part of the Balkan theatre. The evidence from contemporary and more recent documentary sources and from the recent statements of other German staff officers and men, many of whom worked in the same headquarters, has shown that he was a junior staff officer equivalent to a British Army Lieutenant. He was not a member of the German General Staff Corps, which would have carried authority greater than that of his basic Army rank, nor was he a professional intelligence officer.

5.2 His position within the Headquarters Intelligence Branch was that of 03. As such, he was not the Deputy to the Lt. Col. in charge of the Headquarters Intelligence Group but his Assistant. There is no evidence that his position enabled him to intervene with any authority in matters outside his own duties or to alter the decisions of his superiors. He was responsible to the Head of the Intelligence Branch for the provision of information on the previous, current and probable future activities of the Allied forces. This primarily required him to act as a collator, assessor and presenter of such information as was produced by the other personnel in his sub-section and from subordinate headquarters. The interrogation of prisoners of war was one valuable potential source of such information. There is no evidence that his duties involved him personally in interrogations.

5.3 His duties required that he should be well informed about Allied military and political activities, and it is clear that he was well informed on the relationship of these activities to German operations. His knowledge extended to awareness of the decisions that were made as to the eventual disposal of Allied prisoners brought to Salonika for interrogation by the Headquarters' staff, including the transfer of Allied 'commando' prisoners to the SD for disposal, usually by execution, under the so-called 'Commando Order' of 18 October 1942. In this respect, however, his position was no different from that of many others at Army Group Headquarters.

5.4 This available evidence shows that the existence of the 'Commando Order' and its main requirements were general knowledge among officers in the German Army in the Balkans, and among the staff of Headquarters—this was so even down to NCO level. It also shows that the designation of 'commandos' was generally applied by the Germans as a matter of course to Allied personnel involved in 'raiding operations' or in assisting the indigenous partisans: but it was not regarded by the Germans in the Balkan area as an unusual or unwarranted identification in spite of their apparent awareness of the implications for prisoners taken in such operations, namely that they would be passed to the SD with the likelihood of subsequent—illegal—execution.

6. Conclusions regarding Lt. Waldheim's involvement in the particular cases examined

6.1 In the case of the Cephalonia party, there are no grounds for believing that Lt. Waldheim was criminally responsible for Capt. Warren's presumed execution. A statement linking Capt. Warren with 'sabotage' activities was contained in an intelligence report believed to have been written by Lt. Waldheim. This said: 'Warren believed the Greeks were too unreliable to be entrusted with sabotage operations on their own'. However, the statement is not sufficient to amount to instigation or active encouragement of an offence on the part of Lt. Waldheim.

The term linking the party with 'sabotage' activities was used as matter of course in the Balkans to describe the demolition activities of Allied Special Forces and the partisans and had already been used, as had reference to Sonderbehandlung, in earlier reports on this party made during Lt. Waldheim's absence on leave. There is no other evidence that associates him with any decision to execute Capt. Warren.

6.2 In the matter of the Alimnia party, initial designation of the party as 'commandos' and discussion of Sonderbehandlung took place during Lt. Waldheim's absence on leave. There is no evidence that he initiated or authorised the signal to Army Group F requesting instructions on the disposal of the party which led to their transfer to the SD. There is no evidence here of criminal activity by Lt. Waldheim.

6.3 Concerning the Calino party, there is no evidence that Lt. Waldheim personally took the decision concerning the intended disposal of Sgt. Dryden or that he authorised the despatch of the report which he had initialled (and therefore probably drafted) and which included the statement that Sgt. Dryden would be handed over to the SD, an action which was not in fact implemented—Dryden survived the war as a prisoner of war.

6.4 In the case of the Yannina party, there is no evidence to implicate Lt. Waldheim in such illegal treatment of the prisoners as occurred.

6.5 Turning to the cases of other 'commandos' examined, all of whom survived the war, it is clear that Lt. Waldheim was aware that these men were in German hands and knew of their interrogation. But there is no evidence that he was personally involved in the interrogation of any of them, or that he organised, supervised, or controlled such interrogations, or that he was responsible for, or had authority over, those who ran the prisons where they were held. Therefore there is no evidence to implicate Waldheim in any illegal treatment that occurred during these men's captivity.

6.6 In the four cases involving 'non-commando' prisoners which have been examined, there is no evidence to connect Waldheim with Pte. Turton's fate. Of the other three cases, there is no evidence in two of them (the Levitha and Sirina parties) of any illegal activitiy by Lt. Waldheim. In the last case, that of F/Lt. Ogilvie, the actions credited to Lt. Waldheim by F/Lt. Oglivie were apparently intended to aid the prisoner, perhaps saving his life.

6.7 Finally there is the Laterina Case in Italy. Here the discrepancies between the recent allegations and the extensive contemporary evidence, and the lack of any corroboration for the claims, provide no grounds for believing that Lt. Waldheim was involved in the Laterina incident.

7. Waldheim's listing as a War Crimes Suspect

7.1 The evidence from British wartime and early post-war records indicates that Lt. Waldheim was at that time of no war crimes interest to the British authorities, and that he was not personally sought by the United Kingdom for war crimes investigations. His presence in the United Nations War Crimes Commission

(UNWCC) list of war crimes suspects arose from a charge by the Yugoslav authorities in 1948, not from any British investigations. The process by which individuals were added to the UNWCC's lists was heavily reliant on a general assumption that only genuine cases would be submitted, and that the supporting evidence would be genuine and accurate, as the UNWCC's machinery was unable to carry out its own detailed and independent examination of the numerous individual cases submitted to it by member states before deciding to add them to its lists.

7.2 The inclusion of Lt. Waldheim in the Anglo-American and French administered Central Registry of War Criminals and Security Suspects (CROWCASS) list of war crimes suspects again stemmed not from British, American or French investigation and indictment of him as a war crimes suspect but solely because his inclusion in the UNWCC list (as being sought by Yugoslavia) made his addition to the CROWCASS list a matter of routine. CROWCASS was simply a means of registering individuals sought by various Allied countries with a view to aiding their location; it had no judicial or investigative functions and carried out no independent assessment of charges or requests for the listing of individuals.

7.3 The presence of Lt. Waldheim's name on another wartime Allied document has already been explained in Parliament* by the Minister of State for the Armed Forces. The document in question is not a 'List of Top Nazis' or an 'Allied Wanted List'. It is part of a report of the interrogation of a German officer who fell into Allied hands in late 1944 and whose activities in the intelligence field in the Balkans, notably in Salonika and Athens, had naturally brought him into contact with a large number of German Army headquarters officers. During his interrogation he provided the names and a varying amount of detail on these individuals. Lt. Waldheim's name was one of the 238 mentioned by this man.

7.4 The details provided about Waldheim and others such as Lt. Poliza, his colleague, indicated to the wartime Allied counter-intelligence staffs that neither of these two was of any particular significance. They were not included in the Allied register of individuals who were judged to be of interest to the counter-intelligence authorities and whose capture should therefore be reported to the appropriate bodies.

8. **Gaps in the records**

8.1 The contemporary documents which have survived in German and British archives have yielded a fairly comprehensive account of the course of events concerning the cases of the Allied servicemen examined in this Report. But attention has been drawn to the fact that there are gaps in the records, and these call for an explanation.

8.2 In the case of the Alimnia party, some parts of the Foreign Office's file series containing correspondence with the family of one of the servicemen were destroyed some years ago under routine departmental procedures. However copies

* Hansard Commons. 9 March 1988 Written Answer Vol 129. Col 217.

of much of the correspondence which were retained by the family concerned, coupled with surviving War Office papers, have enabled the events of this case (as established by Allied post-war war crimes investigations) to be ascertained. The existence of these contemporary papers demonstrates that, contrary to various recent allegations, there was at no time a policy of systematic destruction of British material relevant to this case with the intention of shielding any individual from being called to account for his actions.

8.3 Similarly, an examination and assessment of contemporary German records, and of the microfilm copies made of these whilst they were in American hands from 1945 until the 1960s, shows that the suggestion that any of them have been destroyed or censored in order to protect Kurt Waldheim for whatever reason is wholly without foundation. The papers relevant to the cases under review that survived the war and fell into Allied hands, especially those regarding the Alimnia party, still survive today and are available for consultation. It has been alleged that the masking of parts of one of these documents was intended to protect wrongdoers. A study of the procedures adopted by the American authorities in the early post-war years shows that in fact the masking was done to conceal the identity of Allied special operations personnel whose names or personal details appeared in the document.

8.4 As distinct from records which were destroyed or masked, a small number of documents in the British records are still not available for public inspection. The reasons for their non-release were given on p 4 above, as is the assurance that their contents have been fully taken into account in this Review.

9. Allegations concerning post-war events

9.1 It has of course not been the practice of successive Governments to comment on speculation or allegations concerning intelligence matters or to discuss its policy concerning elections to the United Nations.

10. Legal conclusions

10.1 Given that much of the evidence has concerned war crimes, it has been necessary to evaluate this evidence from the legal point of view. Therefore, the Review team's historical work has been considered by officers of the Directorate of Army Legal Services who are well versed in the Laws of Armed Conflict and of War Crimes. They reached the conclusion that the evidence available in connection with the cases which they have examined provided no grounds for suggesting that Kurt Waldheim should have faced charges of war crimes in those cases. In the light of his residual responsibility in war crimes matters, the historical Review and annexes were passed to the present Director of Army Legal Services (DALS) who gave the following advice:

> I have considered carefully both the contents of the documents which were submitted and of this Review. At all material times, for the purposes of this Review, the then Lieutenant Waldheim was a mere junior staff officer. There is no evidence here, in my opinion, of relevant delegated executive authority or of any causative, overt act or omission from which his guilt of a war crime may be inferred.

The opinion of DALS endorses the statement made by The Foreign Secretary in 1986 that:

> whatever suspicions the circumstances give rise to concerning the fate of the British servicemen in question, neither the Ministry of Defence's records nor the papers you have provided can be regarded as offering evidence of any criminal activity on the part of Lieutenant Waldheim in relation to those men.

11. **The fate of the Missing British & Commonwealth servicemen**

11.1 It is very much regretted that, in spite of extensive research during this Review, it has not proved possible to obtain any definite evidence as to the final fate of the missing men. Neither careful study of the surviving German documents nor enquiries among surviving Greeks and German military personnel have produced any significant information additional to what was known at the end of the early post-war investigations.

11.2 The execution of such Allied personnel was carried out with as much secrecy as possible. The records of the SD, for example, were apparently most carefully destroyed by their creators before the end of the war and other organisations possibly involved apparently kept no records of such events or again destroyed them. As for personal testimony, the key individuals in the Army Group Headquarters and the SD are dead and those others from the relevant organisations who are still alive and have been traced have been unable to provide any relevant information.

LEGAL BACKGROUND AND ASSESSMENTS

This Section consists of the legal background and assessments of the officers of the Directorate of Army Legal Services, who are well versed in the Laws of Armed Conflict and of War Crimes, and who, with the Director of Army Legal Services (DALS), have examined the historical Review and supporting documents.

WAR CRIMES ASPECTS OF RELEVANT 'COMMANDO' AND RELATED CASES

The 'Commando Order': post-War legal rulings

The status of the 'Commando Order' in law came under court examination in several post-war war crimes trials: most notably during the proceedings of the International Military Tribunal (IMT) at Nuremberg; during a later trial of a number of senior German officers before an American Military Tribunal at Nuremberg, in the case known as the 'High Command Trial'; and in the trial before a British Military court in 1946 of General Von Falkenhorst, the German military commander of Norway.

The IMT in its ruling on the 'Commando Order' stated that:

> This was criminal on its face. It simply directed the slaughter of these sabotage troops.

This ruling endorsed the Allied wartime position as set out in particular by Eisenhower in his March 1945 proclamation. It also implied the rejection of the spurious legal gloss with which Germany sought to argue that Article 23(c) of the Hague Convention for Land Warfare, which stated that it was illegal:

> to kill or wound an enemy who, having laid down his arms or no longer having means of defence, has surrendered at discretion

did not apply to 'commando' operations because this type of covert enemy activity was unknown at the time of the Convention's conclusion and therefore fell outside its provisions.

The transfer of prisoners of war to the SD was similarly ruled to be an illegal act in both the trial of von Falkenhorst, and in the 'High Command Trial' where the Tribunal ruled:

> Orders which provided for the turning over of prisoners of war to the SD, a civilian organization, wherein all accountability for them is shown by the evidence to have been lost, constituted a criminal act, particularly when from the surrounding circumstances and published orders, it must have been suspected or known that the ultimate fate of such prisoners of war was elimination by this murderous organization.

The 'Commando Order' in the Balkans

The contemporary records and testimony of surviving witnesses leave no doubt that the 'Commando Order', if not in all cases its precise wording, was known both to officers and subordinate personnel in the Army Group E Headquarters and in its subordinate formations (such as the division on Rhodes) and that it was well understood what the subsequent fate of those prisoners classified as 'commandos' might be.

Some individuals will have been directly involved with the treatment of 'commandos' and others will have had a more marginal involvement. Given the agreed illegality of the 'Commando Order', the position of those Germans 'involved' in the cases of British 'commandos' in the Balkans (some of whom are believed to have been unlawfully killed) is of particular significance for an examination of the then Lt. Waldheim's role.

Together several of those on Rhodes and in the Army Group E Headquarters were in some way involved with the 'commandos' of the Alimnia party, either in their initial interrogation on Rhodes, or their transportation to Salonika, or in their further interrogation there. Others, although playing no direct part in the interrogation or transfer of the 'commandos', made their existence known to higher authority by transmitting signals containing details of the men's capture. According to some German staff officers, once the news that 'commandos' had been captured had reached 'higher' authority there was little, if any, room for manoeuvre by any individual who wished to thwart the implementation of the 'Commando Order', except at grave risk to himself.

The general treatment of prisoners of war classified as 'commandos'

Apart from any illegal executions, the individual cases examined in the historical section of this Report demonstrate clear breaches of the 1929 Geneva Prisoner of War Convention. For example, pressure was clearly applied by a variety of means to persuade prisoners to provide information beyond that required by Article 5 of the Convention, i.e. true name, rank or service number; while the requirements of Article 8 were not properly observed, namely that a prisoner's capture be notified as soon as possible to his own country through the Protecting Power.

However neither interrogation, nor its organisation were proscribed under international law. Only if illegal methods were used as part of the interrogation process did it become unlawful.

Culpability of staff officers

Post-war Military Tribunals, in considering the question of the personal liability of staff officers who by their acts or omissions may have been deemed to have been involved in the commission of acts contrary to the laws of war, made a number of important rulings and statements. Of especial relevance are those of the Tribunals in 'The Hostages Trial', and the 'High Command Trial'. In the latter it was held that:

> Staff officers, except in limited fields, are not endowed with command authority. Subordinate staff officers normally function through the chiefs of staff. The chief of staff in any command is the closest officer, officially at least, to the commanding officer.

In considering the question of the liability of two senior chiefs of staff during 'The Hostages Trial', the American Military Tribunal ruled as follows:

> The evidence fails to show the result of any action affirmative or passive, on the part of this defendant. His mere knowledge of the happening of unlawful acts does not meet the foregoing requirements of criminal law. He must be one who orders, abets or takes a consenting part in the crime.

It was also held in 'The Hostages Trial', and in the case of 'Harukei Isayama and Others', that a staff officer cannot be held responsible for the outcome of his commander's orders which he approves from the point of view of form and issues on the commander's behalf. It is of interest that Foertsch, who was Chief of Staff of Army Group E when the 'Commando Order' was issued, and von Geitner, who as Chief of Staff initialled or signed orders issued by his commander for the shooting of hostages and reprisal prisoners, were acquitted by the American Military Tribunal in 'The Hostages Trial'. On the other hand, Harukei Isayama, who as Chief of Staff played a personal and active part in the organisation of an unlawful trial of American airmen, was convicted by the American Military Tribunal.

Another defendant was found not guilty

> not having been shown to have taken any consenting part in illegal acts, 'coupled with the nature and responsibilities of his position and the want of authority on his part to prevent the execution of the unlawful acts charged'.

While there is no suggestion that any of these cases provide Chiefs of Staff or other staff officers with immunity from prosecution for criminal acts, they established more clearly the level of involvement required for something to be deemed a criminal act. Further they demonstrate the distinction between knowledge of, and criminal involvement in such illegal acts.

Legal findings in the cases under review

a. The Cephalonia Case

In the case of the presumed execution of Capt. D. A. La Touche Warren in May 1944, there is no evidence that a formal war crimes investigation was instituted. Although there was a suggestion within the local SOE organisation that the commander of the prison be sought, there was apparently no approach by SOE to the war crimes investigators for the case to be followed up.

The only evidence of a possible order concerning Capt. Warren's disposal comes from the signal of Army Group F of 28 March 1944 (see Chapter 6 of historical section of Report) which mentions Sonderbehandlung after interrogation for the whole Group of prisoners.

Lt. Waldheim's involvement

Lt. Waldheim's involvement in this case can only have begun after his return from leave on 16 or 17 April 1944 by which time the above signal had already been passed to the OKW. His personal involvement can be seen in the report of 8 May 1944 believed to have been drafted by Lt. Waldheim which detailed the information gained from the interrogations of members of the party including Capt. Warren. The report said that 'Warren believed that the Greeks were too unreliable to be entrusted with sabotage operations on their own'. This report and the relevance of the use of the term 'sabotage' have been examined. It is considered that there is no evidence of any act by Lt. Waldheim that made him liable for prosecution on war crimes charges in this case.

b. The Alimnia Case

A formal war crimes investigation was initiated at the end of 1946. The course of this investigation is covered in detail in Chapter 7 of the historical section of this Report. In summary, the investigators were able to locate and interrogate a number of German officers and men who had clearly been involved with the 'commandos' on Rhodes, in reporting their capture, in their interrogation and their transfer to Salonika. There is no evidence that any of these individuals was considered because of his actions to be culpable for the presumed later murder of the prisoners concerned. Nor is there evidence that any action was considered against any of these Germans for the lesser infringements, notably of Article 8 of the 1929 Prisoner of War Convention mentioned earlier, which required the notification of prisoners' capture as soon as possible, despite the fact that their failure to comply with this requirement could be said to form an integral part of the procedure for the implementation of the 'Commando Order', rather than the men's treatment as ordinary prisoners of war.

The war crimes team were apparently concerned to apprehend and bring to trial those individuals within the theatre command structure with executive authority directly implicating them in the assumed illegal disposal of the prisoners.

Within the Army Group E Headquarters, attention focussed on Lt. Col. Warnstorff, and Maj. Hammer. Neither was traced, but they were wanted for questioning; there is no evidence that either was considered as a potential accused. Two suspects however were identified: Lt. Col. von Harling and Capt. Merram both from the Army Group F Headquarters. They were arrested and interrogated but no war crimes trial took place under the Royal Warrant prior to the cessation of such trials. The two men were then transferred to Control Commission Germany (CCG) custody, but although the existence of machinery to prosecute before CCG courts was in place, the surviving documentary evidence indicates that no trial was held under CCG auspices and that both men were soon released. The reason for this was a lack of sufficient evidence to sustain a viable case against them.

Lt. Waldheim's involvement

Current research shows that Lt. Waldheim was absent from the Headquarters of Army Group E on leave in Austria from March until 16 or 17 April 1944. He was therefore not involved in the early action in this case during which period the existence of the men was reported up to the highest level—the German Armed Forces High Command (OKW) and possibly even Hitler—and a Wehrmachtbericht had already also been issued indicating that the men were considered to be 'commandos' as defined in the 'Commando Order'.

While it is clear that following his return to the Headquarters Lt. Waldheim was aware of the existence of the 'commandos' and their intended fate when this was ordered by Army Group F, it is considered that the evidence indicates only a limited personal involvement by him in the case and reveals nothing to suggest that he committed any criminal acts.

The allegation against Lt. Waldheim is that he was responsible for a signal sent on 26 April 1944 from the staff branch to which he belonged, addressed to HQ Army Group F saying: 'Further interrogation of English Alimnia commandos without result. Request decision on whether the prisoners now to be handed over to SD'. It is unlikely that Waldheim's authorship of this signal could be proved and even if it could, the issuing of orders on behalf of the commander does not of itself engage legal responsiblility. Indeed the issuing of this signal was one stage further removed from the activity of von Geitner, acquitted in 'The Hostages Trial', since it merely enquired about whether prisoners should be handed to the SD and did not pass on an order for execution.

It is considered that this view is consistent with the decisions of the post-war war crimes investigators who examined this case. Lt. Waldheim's limited involvement was less than that of the German officers on Rhodes who were closely involved in the 'commandos' initial identification, interrogation and handling yet were not considered by the war crimes team to be perpetrators of any illegal acts.

c. The Yannina Case

A formal war crimes investigation was initiated and the evidence from the ex-prisoners identified the NCO Stoffberg from the Geheime Feldpolizei (GFP) prison, who it was felt was primarily responsible for the prisoners' ill-treatment. However he did not fall into Allied hands and therefore no further action could be taken.

Lt. Waldheim's involvement

A report on the men's capture was sent to the Ic/AO Branch in Salonika. It was Lt. Waldheim's job to be familiar with these reports and with the results of any interrogations, whether by subordinate units, the GFP or by the Army Group itself. But there is no evidence to link Lt. Waldheim personally with the men's interrogation: some of his former colleagues have testified to conducting at least some of these interrogations while denying any participation by him. There is also no evidence that he was personally involved in deciding interrogation procedures.

With reference to the basic treatment of the prisoners and the general conditions in the GFP prison, there is no evidence that Lt. Waldheim ever visited the GFP prison or had any responsibility for the GFP: this lay with his superior Lt. Col. Warnstorff with the day to day responsibility delegated to the AO Maj. Hammer in conjunction with the GFP's own commander.

It is concluded therefore that there is no evidence of criminal actions by Lt. Waldheim in relation to this case.

d. The Calino Case

This was initially identified as a possible war crimes case by the American authorities examining captured German records. However it must be presumed that enquiries soon established that Sgt. Dryden had not been executed as a 'commando' but had survived the war, as the case was not pursued by the British authorities.

Significantly, when the German report was identified by the US war crimes investigators examining the German Army records they considered that the individuals concerned in this proposed breach of the law were the Commanding Generals of Army Groups F & E, and the Chief of Staff of Army Group F.

Lt. Waldheim's involvement

In this instance it is believed that Lt. Waldheim initialled the report, indicating that the facts and interpretations therein which he had provided and drafted were correct. The report said 'Sgt. John Dryden born 25 October 1919 in Newcastle, wounded, flown to Athens on 5 July will be handed over to SD in accordance with the Führerbefehl'. Lt. Waldheim must have been aware of the implications of the proposal regarding Dryden's disposal, but since Dryden survived the war, any allegation against Lt. Waldheim could only be of involvement in an attempt to commit a war crime. To prove such a charge it would be necessary to show that Lt. Waldheim had intended to cause the death of this prisoner rather than that he had simply recorded the facts including the decision, made elsewhere, that the captive was to be passed to the SD. There is no evidence that Lt. Waldheim authorised the statement regarding the proposed fate of Dryden, or that he had any authority to do so or could officially influence it in any way. Therefore there is no available evidence to support the allegation of criminal activity by Lt. Waldheim in this case.

e. The Leros prisoners

Of these cases only that of Flt. Lt. Ogilvie links Lt. Waldheim to allegations of war crimes. In his recent testimony he states that Lt. Waldheim escorted him from the transit camp to the headquarters at Salonika and that during the flight Lt. Waldheim asked for the prisoners' identity discs which were then replaced by some from the corpses of soldiers who had been serving in open combat units. There is no corroboration for this allegation, indeed the surrounding circumstances point against it, but, taken at face value, Ogilvie's evidence indicates a violation of Article 6 of the 1929 Prisoners of War Convention. However, the implication is that by changing the identity discs Lt. Waldheim saved Ogilvie's life. In those circumstances, even if corroborative evidence existed a prosecution would be inappropriate.

f. Pte. Turton's death

This was carefully investigated and the identities of several suspects established, all of them SD, SS or GFP, but apparently none of them fell into British or Allied hands and no further investigation could therefore take place. There is no evidence of any involvment of Lt. Waldheim in this case.

g. The Laterina Case

This case was carefully investigated by British, Canadian and American war crimes teams and the case was listed by the United Kingdom with the UNWCC. However it appears that none of the accused fell into Allied hands and therefore no trial could take place.

These contemporary investigations reveal no evidence of any involvement by Lt. Waldheim in this case or of his presence at the end of the affair.

In view of the discrepancies in the evidence highlighted in this Review, and of the absence of any evidence to corroborate the one allegation, it is considered that there is insufficient evidence of any participation by Lt. Waldheim in any illegal activity.

h. Other cases examined in the Review

Although there were some infringements of the Geneva Convention concerning the treatment of some of these men, there is no evidence to suggest that Lt. Waldheim was involved personally in the commission or authorisation of any illegal actions in relation to them.

Conclusions

From the examination of the evidence concerning the cases of British 'commandos' held prisoner in the area under the control of Army Group E, it is clear that Lt. Waldheim must have been aware of the 'Commando Order' and its implications and also of the existence of these British prisoners and of their interrogation.

However, in the light of the evidence examined during the Review and the test laid down in 'The Hostages Trial' that mere knowledge is insufficient and that the accused must 'be the one who orders, abets or takes a consenting part in the crime', it is concluded that there is no evidence that Lt. Waldheim committed criminal acts in these cases.

In conclusion the Director of Army Legal Services (DALS) has stated:

> I have considered carefully both the contents of the documents which were submitted and of this Review. At all material times for the purposes of this Review, the then Lieutenant Waldheim was a mere junior staff officer. There is no evidence here, in my opinion, of relevant delegated executive authority or of any causative, overt act or omission from which his guilt of a war crime may be inferred.

HISTORICAL REPORT

Master
Professor Sir Harry Hinsley, O.B.E., M.A., F.B.A.

The Master's Lodge
St John's College
Cambridge CB2 1TP

5 July, 1989

Dear Minister of State,

My brief was to scrutinise the results of the research carried out for this Report in the Ministry of Defence, with the assistance of the Foreign Office, in order to ensure its objectivity and thoroughness.

In carrying it out, my first concern has been to establish that the Report has examined all the records, whether in the possession of H.M. Government or otherwise available for inspection, that might conceivably have a bearing on the subject. To the best of my knowledge and ability, I am satisfied that this is the case; and I am further satisfied that no pertinent evidence in these records has been overlooked in the body of the Report.

This evidence is as far as possible reproduced as documents in annexes. For reasons explained in the Report an exception to this practice has had to be made for a small number of documents in the British archives. The authors of the Report have had access to these documents, however, as to all other British records that might be relevant, and they have provided either an extract from them or the gist of the contents. I have studied such documents as cannot be reproduced as annexes either in full or at all, and I am satisfied that when summarising or drawing conclusions from them the authors of the Report have properly represented their contents.

Turning from the thoroughness of the Report to the matter of its objectivity, I am able to extend to the Report as a whole the above assurance about the interpretation placed on the small number of restricted documents. My enquiries in this direction have addressed two questions: whether the allegations made against Kurt Waldheim in relation to the treatment accorded to British and Commonwealth prisoners of war, and against H.M. Government in the form of suspicions voiced about its earlier concealment of information, have been accurately recapitulated in the Report; and whether the conclusions it reaches regarding these allegations fairly reflect the evidence, negative and positive, which the authors have assembled in the course of their exhaustive enquiry. In my judgment the answer to each of these questions is in the affirmative.

Yours sincerely,

F. H. Hinsley

The Hon. A. G. Hamilton,
Minister of State for the Armed Forces,
Ministry of Defence,
Main Building,
Whitehall,
London SW1.

Introduction

This report is concerned only with cases involving British servicemen captured by the Germans in Greece and the Greek Islands, in the area under the command of the German Army Group E between October 1943 and October 1944. These, it has been alleged, demonstrate or point strongly to the probability that the then Lt. Waldheim engaged in acts amounting to war crimes. The allegations concerning the then Lt. Waldheim in respect of British servicemen have come from a number of sources including Members of Parliament, international organisations, ex-servicemen and other individuals and through the media. These allegations have been collated into the list in Chapter 2.

The historical background to these cases is set out in Chapter 3 which describes the general nature of the operations undertaken by the British servicemen and the organisation of the opposing German forces. The details of the Headquarters in which Lt. Waldheim worked are given in Chapter 4.

Chapter 5 summarises the essential aspects and application of Hitler's Order—the 'Commando Order'—which stipulated the elimination of Allied servicemen engaged in activities identified as 'commando' operations.

The details of individual cases are discussed in Chapters 6–10, with particular reference to any involvement of Lt. Waldheim. A summary of this involvement is provided in Chapter 11.

Finally, Chapter 12 reviews the evidence relating to the allegations that relevant documents may have been tampered with or destroyed. A summary of the documentary and other sources used in this Review is given below.

Sources

In the course of its work the Review team has consulted many documents from a number of archives, official and private bodies, and private individuals. Generous assistance has been received from a number of other countries, including archives in America, Germany, Greece, Austria and Sweden. Especial thanks are due both to the US National Archives, particularly Robert Wolfe, Director of the Captured German Records Staff, and to Dr. Kehrig, the Director, and his staff of the German Federal Archives, Military Division at Freiburg, for their assistance and for permission to reproduce copies of their records in this Report. Crown Copyright material in the Public Record Office is reproduced by permission of the Controller of Her Majesty's Stationery Office. The assistance is also gratefully acknowledged of the Office of Special Investigations, US Department of Justice; Thames Television and Jack Saltman the producer of the Thames Television programme 'Waldheim A Case to Answer?' and his research staff; the World Jewish Congress in New York; the Greek Red Cross; Gerald Fleming, British member of the International Commission of Historians appointed by the Austrian Government; Mr Andrew Tuckey; and The Hon. C. M. Woodhouse; as well as the contributions of a large number of other individuals and organisations who have provided information and have answered questions. All these contributions are gratefully acknowledged. The interpretation of the material and information provided has been a matter for the Review team.

The Review team have not necessarily sought to question some individuals who have already provided testimony for other investigations into this general subject such as the Austrian Commission and the Thames Television programme, as their material has kindly been made available to the team.

The Review team has been given unlimited use of British official records, both those within the public domain and those still in Government hands. The latter include those that have not yet been released to the public domain through the Public Record Office and those from certain intelligence agencies, which are unlikely to be released for reasons of security.

As many as possible of the most important documents have been reproduced as Annexes and their source references are listed on the fiche. Sources for statements in the text which are not supported by Annexes are referenced at the end of each chapter. It has not been felt necessary therefore to produce a bibliography. This would be of inordinate length if it were to reflect accurately the thousands of files examined in War Office, Foreign Office and Treasury Solicitor's papers in the Public Record Office, and those still in Government hands, as well as those examined elsewhere.

In order to assist the reader translations have been provided for those documents produced as Annexes which are not in English and where the meaning is not immediately clear. However the work of the Review has been based on the original text and not on the translations.

Finally attention is drawn to the statement by Professor Sir Harry Hinsley, Master of St. John's College, Cambridge who agreed to scrutinise the results of the historical section of the Review in order to ensure its objectivity and thoroughness.

Chapter 1: Terms of reference

In 1986, following Parliamentary interest in claims that the fate of certain British servicemen who fell into German hands during the Second World War was linked with the wartime service there of Kurt Waldheim, the Government decided that Ministry of Defence records should be examined to establish whether they contained any relevant information. The review also examined copies of other material, primarily from contemporary German documents now available either in the United States of America or in the Federal Republic of Germany, which were passed to the British Government by interested parties.

This review found no evidence of criminal activity by the then Lt. Waldheim in relation to the cases examined. Its conclusions were passed on by the Foreign Secretary in letters to those Members of Parliament who had raised the subject.

Early in 1988 the Report was published of the International Commission of Historians established by the Austrian Government to look into allegations of the involvement of Kurt Waldheim in war crimes in the Balkan theatre during the Second World War. This stated that:

> The Commission has reached the following conclusion: It emerges from this course of events that Waldheim was well aware of the matter of the commandos, for a number of documents still in existence relating to commando prisoners, interrogations and the handing over of such prisoners to the SD [Nazi Party Security Service] passed over his desk. By initialling such documents, First Lieutenant Waldheim had knowledge of them and the course of events . . . .
>
> . . . The passing on of interrogation records of statements made by Allied commandos was causally related to the latter's fate, as laid down in general terms in Hitler's Commando Order of 18 October 1942. Involvement of this kind can be described as obeying an order in clear awareness of the fact that the order is criminal in intent.

In the light of the report, which had had access to a wider range of sources than the Ministry of Defence, Her Majesty's Government decided that the Ministry should review the results of its 1986 work.

The Prime Minister said, in a written answer in the House of Commons on 16 February 1988:

> We are reviewing the results of investigations carried out in 1986 by the Ministry of Defence into the fate of captured British servicemen, including those mentioned by my hon. Friend, in the light of the report of the International Commission of Historians on the wartime record of President Waldheim. I would remind the House that we have taken the allegations concerning Dr Waldheim very seriously, particularly those concerning British servicemen, and that our thorough investigation of British official records has found no evidence to substantiate the allegations. As we have said before, we remain ready to examine all new information. (Hansard Commons. Vol 127. col 519)

Later, in a written answer on 29 February 1988, Mr Ian Stewart, then Minister of State for the Armed Forces, said:

> As announced by my right hon. Friend the Prime Minister on 16 February, the Ministry of Defence, in conjunction with other interested Departments, is conducting a review of the results of the investigations which it carried out in 1986 into the fate of captured British servicemen and the involvement, if any, of the then Lieutenant Waldheim in the light of the report of the independent International Commission of Historians. The commission had access to a wider range of sources than was available to the team which carried out the investigation in 1986, and we therefore wish to reconsider the question taking account of the commission's findings.
>
> It is our intention that the review, which will re-examine all aspects relating to the fate of the captured British servicemen, should be as thorough and comprehensive as possible. Anyone who has concrete evidence that might be relevant to the review is encouraged to submit it to the Ministry of Defence for examination by the review team.
>
> The review will be pursued as quickly as is consistent with proper consideration of the evidence and the need for accuracy. When it has been completed, it is the intention that a report should be published.
>
> I am grateful to Professor Sir Harry Hinsley, the Master of St John's College, Cambridge, for agreeing to scrutinise the results of the review in order to ensure its objectivity and thoroughness.
>
> My right hon. Friend the Secretary of State has asked the review team to report to me on the conduct of the review. I very much hope that anyone who has information to give will do so without delay so that the review can be completed as soon as possible. (Hansard Commons. Vol 128. cols 418–419).

These were the initial terms of reference for the Review. During its course a number of related points concerning Lt. Waldheim's wartime service and this country's knowledge of this were raised and these have been investigated.

Chapter 2: Allegations concerning Kurt Waldheim

There have been a number of allegations against Kurt Waldheim concerning his wartime service in the Balkans. Some of them are outside the scope of the Review as they do not involve British personnel. Although he was serving in that theatre from 1942 onwards, the allegations that as a result of his duties he was involved with British servicemen relate to the period from October 1943 when he joined the staff of the Headquarters of the German Army Group E based in Salonika in northern Greece, to late 1944, when that Headquarters withdrew north into Yugoslavia.

The key allegations against Kurt Waldheim that are of relevance to this Review are that, as an officer in the Headquarters Staff of Army Group E at Salonika during the year 1944:

a. he was personally involved in the interrogation of, or in the organising and control of matters relating to a number of British servicemen held as prisoners by the Germans—notably the men captured off the island of Cephalonia, on the island of Alimnia, near Yannina, and on the island of Calino—and, therefore, that he was culpable of any mistreatment of British prisoners which occurred.

b. he was personally involved in the decision and perhaps gave or relayed the orders to transfer British prisoners to the Nazi Party's Sicherheitsdienst (SD) for Sonderbehandlung under Hitler's 'Commando Order', which in some cases resulted in their execution (as is believed to have been the fate of the missing Alimnia men and Capt. Warren of the Cephalonia party).

c. in a report on Capt. Warren (the leader of the Cephalonia party) he falsely classified him as a 'saboteur' with the consequence that Capt. Warren was considered to fall into the category of individuals liable for Sonderbehandlung and was executed.

d. as the British servicemen in sub-paragraphs a.–c. above were subjected to treatment that violated the laws of war, and because Lt. Waldheim was involved in or responsible for such treatment, he is therefore a War Criminal—being in these cases at least an 'accessory' even if not a 'principal'.

e. he was personally involved in some manner in the illegal shooting of a number of Allied prisoners of war from the Laterina Camp in Italy.

In support of these charges, other claims have been made concerning Lt. Waldheim's role and authority within the Headquarters that suggest that:

f. he was an important and powerful staff officer whose authority far out-reached his military rank, whose views and suggestions carried great weight with his superiors even up to the Commander-in-Chief, and who was able to influence their decisions in areas outside his official concern, making him to some extent responsible for the results of such decisions.

g. because of his position within Army Group E's Headquarters, he was of such value as a potential source of intelligence that he was actively sought by the Allies and was placed on an Allied 'Wanted List' during the war.

It has further been asserted that:

h. Lt. Waldheim's wartime role in the Balkans was known to the British authorities; and that he had been accurately identified in British records and, as these included evidence of his culpability in relation to war crimes against British personnel, he was noted as a war crimes suspect; and that these matters were known during the war and the immediate post-war years, as well as in 1970 when he first stood for the post of Secretary General of the United Nations.

i. the above mentioned records were deliberately destroyed or concealed to protect Lt. Waldheim because he had been of assistance to British intelligence.

Chapter 3: Historical background

This chapter provides the essential information about the Allied operations in the Balkans and the general organisation of the German Army at the time, with particular reference to the Balkans.

Allied operations in the Balkans

Following the German invasions of Yugoslavia and Greece in the spring of 1941, British forces were sent to Greece to help oppose the German forces. However the Allied efforts were unsuccessful and the Germans and their Italian Axis partner occupied both the mainland countries and the dependent Adriatic, Aegean and Mediterranean islands. Turkey remained a neutral state and officially uninvolved with either the Axis or the Allied causes.

After the withdrawal of the British and Commonwealth regular forces, some of the local population formed indigenous resistance groups to oppose the occupation troops. These were generally called partisans by the Allies, but the Germans called them 'bands' with the implication that their activities were unlawful within the then existing Laws of Warfare. The Allies sought to encourage both the growth and effectiveness of these groups, primarily through Force 133—the Middle Eastern branch of the Special Operations Executive (SOE)—the organisation created by the United Kingdom for this purpose. The Force 133 personnel in Greece were grouped into a body known initially as the British, later the Allied, Military Mission (AMM). Apart from advice on operational matters, the AMM helped the resistance with specialist instruction and training, particularly in demolition techniques, and also by providing arms, food, clothing etc., mainly by airdrops.

Other organisations within the area included MI9, responsible for organising escape routes, to help Allied personnel in enemy territory either to evade capture or to make good their escape, aided by elements of A Force with a similar role, and the Inter-Services Liaison Department (ISLD), an intelligence gathering body.

Following the Italian state's surrender and switch to the Allied cause in September 1943, the British sought to exploit this by landing on a number of the Aegean and Dodecanese islands whose Italian garrisons either did not oppose or actively supported the Allied actions. These operations brought large numbers of British troops into the eastern Mediterranean and resulted in fierce fighting with the German forces there.

By the end of 1943 the Germans had succeeded in ousting the Allies from the Aegean islands they had occupied following the Italian surrender. The Allies however were anxious to persuade the Germans to keep strong forces in the area, thus aiding the forthcoming Allied operations 'Overlord' and 'Anvil' in France and Russian operations on the Eastern front. As part of the overall Allied strategy, therefore, it was important that some military pressure should be maintained on the Germans in the Balkans to support a deceptive Allied threat to the area.

A valuable part of the Allied 'pressure', notably on the mainland including Greece, was the continuing existence of the local resistance forces which it was hoped to expand through the efforts of the AMM. On the Aegean and other islands, apart from facing the threat of guerrilla activity, the German garrisons were largely dependent on sea traffic for major re-supply and in the face of attacks by Allied submarines and aircraft, coastal traffic by caiques and other small boats less vulnerable to these forms of attack grew in importance.

The Allied response to the German use of coastal vessels was to intensify attacks on this traffic while continuing operations against the island garrisons themselves. The Allied forces were expected to:

a. capture or destroy coastal shipping.

b. attack land bases, including key points such as supply dumps, radar, radio and telegraph posts and defence positions.

c. set up observation posts on islands to locate suitable targets.

As part of these operations the Allies had set up small forward bases on islands close to or inside Turkish territorial waters, which were thus less exposed to German attack. The Turkish authorities 'turned a blind eye' to this Allied action.

The military land forces operating in the area consisted of the Raiding Forces in conjunction with the Royal Navy's Coastal Forces Eastern Mediterranean, which incorporated the Anglo-Hellenic Schooner Flotillas*.

The component parts of the Raiding Forces were the Special Boat Squadron† (SBS), which was by then part of the Special Air Service and the Greek Sacred Squadron, comprising Greek Military volunteers trained for special operations.

The Long Range Desert Group, which had also been involved in operations in the Aegean at the end of 1943, was transferred to Italy, as was the newly raised Raiding Support Regiment (RSR), both coming under command of the Central Mediterranean Theatre. But the RSR operated on the Greek mainland, largely under the operational control of Force 133. Movement to the area of operations was carried out by air with a parachute landing or by boat, the latter method being especially suitable for the insertion and extraction of large bodies of men or quantities of supplies.

In the spring of 1944 a special body (Force 266) was established to control special operations in Yugoslavia by forces based in Italy and to support Force 133 personnel. This replaced what had previously been known as Advanced Force 133.

All these units were proper military bodies of the British Armed Forces or in the case of SOE, staffed by members of these Forces. However their role and method of operation and their somewhat 'ad hoc' nature and existence led to their being generally considered as 'Special Forces' as against conventional units or those

* The title of this force was changed from the Levant Schooner Flotilla to that given above in the spring of 1944.
† This unit had several changes to its title during this period. Until April 1943 it had been the Special Boat Section; from April 1943 until May 1944 it was the Special Boat Squadron; then it became the Special Boat Service.

engaged in what the Germans considered to be conventional warfare.‡ Their members, as soldiers operating in uniform as part of a formally organised military body, were entitled to the status of prisoners of war if captured and to the protection of the Geneva Convention of 1929 governing the treatment of such individuals.

From the end of 1943 Allied operations within the Mediterranean, including the Balkans, were under the overall command of the Supreme Allied Commander Mediterranean Theatre who from 8 January 1944 was General Wilson. Operations in Italy and the Eastern Mediterranean were the direct responsibility respectively of the Commander-in-Chief Allied Armies in Italy (General Alexander) and the Service Commanders-in-Chief, Middle East in Cairo. Land operations in the Balkans, both on the mainland and on the Aegean islands, were initially controlled by the General Headquarters Middle East Forces (in Cairo) which was in a position to co-ordinate military operations with those of other agencies, mainly from the intelligence field. Special operations however were co-ordinated by a new HQ Special Operations Mediterranean (SOM), also based in Cairo from April 1944. The overall picture is depicted on the chart at Annex 1.

German Forces

Under Adolf Hitler, the Supreme Commander of the German Armed Forces, was the German Armed Forces High Command—Oberkommando der Wehrmacht (OKW)—headed by Field Marshal Keitel. The OKW exercised central control of operations through the Armed Forces Operations Staff—Wehrmachtsführungsstab (W.F.St.)—with Colonel-General Jodl as Chief of Staff. Under him, and of especial importance, was the Joint Planning Staff commanded by General Warlimont. There were also subordinate single Service commands: for the Army this was the Oberkommando des Heeres (OKH) (Annex 2).

The Army command chain passed down through Army Group or Army Headquarters to subordinate corps and divisions. Within the OKH itself there were also departments dealing with specific areas: one department of particular significance was that responsible for the evaluation and dissemination of information on Western Allied forces—Foreign Armies West, Fremde Heere West (Fr. H. West).

Intelligence was co-ordinated at OKW by the Head of the Abwehr which, despite its title strictly implying counter-intelligence was engaged in all forms of intelligence. Intelligence would be passed from Abwehr sources to the evaluating bodies in the OKH and through them to the operational net and down to subordinate headquarters. However, the Abwehr also had its own organisation within each area and this could be used to pass information to the neighbouring military headquarters (Annex 3).

‡ Throughout the Review the term 'commando' is used to denote members of the Special Forces and special organisations. The Special Forces concerned were not strictly speaking 'commandos' (i.e. members of the Army or Royal Marine Commando Units) but, as the Germans used the word, it has been adopted as a generic term to denote the cases and types of operations covered by this Review. The individual constituent units or bodies are still indicated where appropriate.

Within the Balkans the original Army Command based at Arsakli just outside Salonika was Army Group E—Heeresgruppe E (H.Gr.E.). From 26 August 1943 it was subordinated to a new Headquarters (Army Group F) based at Belgrade in Yugoslavia, the commander of which was also designated Commander-in-Chief South East—Oberbefehlshaber (O.B) Südost. In many matters Army Group F was subordinated directly to the OKW. Army Group E was now responsible only for operations in Greece and the Aegean islands: its subordinate formations consisted of several Corps and some independent divisions on Crete and Rhodes (Annex 4).

While the Commander-in-Chief South-East had authority over all the military units in the area, the administration, as was the German practice, was the responsibility of the Military Commander. He was primarily concerned with the maintenance of security and order as well as the general control of the population and the economic life of the country. The Military Commander for Greece was based at Athens. On matters concerning policy he usually took his orders from OKH but as commander of the security and police forces allotted to him—usually German police units and security divisions from the Army plus locally raised auxiliaries—he was tactically subordinate to the Commander-in-Chief of his area. Therefore he also worked closely with Army Group E at Salonika.

Within the Armed Forces in the area was an organisation called the Geheime Feldpolizei (GFP)—the Secret Field Police—which operated primarily as a military security force. Apart from the Armed Forces, there were also the elements of the Nazi party's own organisation, the SS, which by this time had its own military formations (the Waffen SS) some of which were serving in the Balkans. However the most important part of the Nazi and SS organisation from the point of view of this Review was the SD. This was originally formed as the intelligence agency of the Nazi party. However it became closely involved with the Sicherheitspolizei (SIPO)—the Security Police, which consisted of the Criminal Police (Kripo) and the Secret State Police (Gestapo)—in the task of discovering threats to the security of the Nazi system. This was especially true within occupied territories, where the SIPO and the SD operated in combined commands.

The functions of these bodies were primarily to ensure the internal security of the area especially by gathering intelligence on, tracking down, and helping to eliminate 'subversive' elements. This included work against partisans and their supporters. In general the SIPO and SD were ruthless in their dealings with opponents.

The SIPO and SD co-existed with the Military organisation within occupied areas, but were partially independent of it in terms of command and control structure. Their activities were ultimately controlled in such areas by the SS and Police Commander. Although officially under the Military Commander for Greece, he also had his own chain of command which went to the Reichssicherheitshauptamt (RSHA), the Reich Security Headquarters in Germany (Annex 5).

Chapter 4: The Organisation of the Intelligence Branch (Ic/AO) in Army Group E Headquarters

Introduction

The following examination of the status of Lt. Waldheim and his official functions within the Headquarters of Army Group E is concerned primarily with the period from late 1943 until October 1944, when the Army Group and its Headquarters withdrew northwards into Yugoslavia, and seeks to clarify his duties, his status and the scope of his authority, if any, for decision making and the issuing of orders.

The evidence rests mainly on surviving contemporary documents including general Allied evaluations of German Army headquarters organisation and procedure. However later statements made by Wehrmacht personnel who served alongside Kurt Waldheim in the Headquarters of Army Group E or who had other relevant experience are taken into account. Although memories can be fallible after so many years, these statements are valuable because the information available in the surviving contemporary documents is limited. The more recent researches of others in this field have also been noted.

Organisation of Army Group E Headquarters

Army Group E HQ was headed by the Commander-in-Chief—Gen. Löhr. Under his Chief of Staff, the Headquarters staff were organised into three main areas: Operations, Supply and Personnel matters. Within the Operations area were three separate Branches: the Operations Branch, the Intelligence Branch and the Special Staff Branch.

During the period in question the main elements of the Headquarters of Army Group E were based at Arsakli, some 5kms outside Salonika, on high ground overlooking the town. It was sometimes called 'Panorama' because of the good view. The Headquarters occupied a number of buildings, among them the Villa Heitmann and the buildings of the pre-war American College. Among the elements at Arsakli were the Operations Branch (Ia) and the joint Intelligence and Counter-Intelligence Branch (Ic/AO). Other less important parts of the Headquarters were based in Salonika and communicated with Arsakli by telephone. The Headquarters at Arsakli was apparently self-contained in that it had its own accommodation and messing facilities, and was therefore to a large extent independent of the town.

From October 1943 Waldheim—now an Oberleutnant (equivalent to a British Army Lieutenant)—served in the Ic/AO Branch. According to Allied wartime and immediate post-war studies of the German Staff system, the whole Ic/AO Branch usually consisted of some nine officers plus NCOs and other ranks, and this seems to tally quite closely with documentary evidence concerning Army Group E. The overall composition of the HQ and the place of the Ic/AO Branch is shown on the attached chart. (Annex 6).

The Ic/AO Branch was responsible for the provision of intelligence on the enemy's forces, their organisation, equipment, actions and assessed intentions. This information was passed to the Ia—the Operations Branch—who were responsible for the control of the operations of the Germans and their allies. The contributions of the Ic/AO Branch was of great importance in the evaluation of the best course of action in the light of perceived enemy activity, but the control and issuing of orders on operational matters was the responsibility and prerogative of the Army Commander and his operations staff.

The Head of the whole Ic/AO Branch was Maj. (later Lt. Col.) H. Warnstorff, and as such he had the title 'Ic'. He was a professional Staff Officer and a member of the German General Staff Corps, hence the letters 'i.G.' after his name. Membership of the General Staff Corps gave Lt. Col. Warnstorff authority and commensurate status in relation to others greater than was strictly conferred by his army rank: in an army headquarters a Lt. Col. who was a General Staff Officer might well have under his command higher ranking officers such as full Colonels who were not General Staff Officers. Within the HQ itself Warnstorff was the nominated deputy for the Lt. Col. heading the Operations Branch (the Ia) who was also a General Staff Officer.

As a part of his Branch's intelligence collation and assessment responsiblities, the Ic was personally involved in discussions with other senior officers both of the operations staff and from the other forces involved in the control of the occupied territory.

The organisation of the Ic/AO Branch within Army Group E's Headquarters is set out in a contemporary German document dating from December 1943. This provides an outline of the duties of the different sections and sub-sections within the Branch (Annex 7). This distribution of duties seems to conform with the general model set out in the German Army General Staff Handbook (Annex 8). A further contemporary general statement on the branch's tasks is at Annex 9.

Lt. Col. Warnstorff was responsible for both parts of the Ic/AO Branch; his Deputy (Vertreter) was the AO (Abwehr-Offizier)—Counter-Intelligence Officer—Maj. F. W. Hammer who ran the AO section. The question of the extent of Warnstorff's direct supervision and control of the work of the AO is considered more fully later in this Chapter.

In general terms the division of responsibilities between the Ic and the AO sections was that the Ic section dealt with military intelligence relating to strategic, including political, operational and tactical matters, while the AO section was concerned primarily with counter-intelligence duties. The duties of the AO section included the collection of intelligence on the internal security situation relevant to the maintenance of a comprehensive picture of enemy activity and required co-operation with other elements in the internal security field, notably the various police and SS organisations as well as input from other intelligence agencies. The Ic's duties in relation to the drafting of operational orders was it seems confined to providing the descriptive section on the 'enemy' forces.

The 03 Sub-Section

Within the Ic section there were a number of individual sub-sections responsible for particular aspects of work, one of which we have for clarity called the 03 sub-section.

Oberleutnant Waldheim's post within the Ic/AO Branch was that of 03. He was one of several Ordonnanz Offiziere within the Headquarters. An Ordonnanz Offizier was in effect an assistant to a senior staff officer.* In Army Group E, the 03 and 05 worked for the Ic/AO Branch.

When the 05 post fell vacant in February 1944, the duties were shared out among the other junior officers in the 03 sub-section.

As the 03, Waldheim was the assistant to the Ic but only for the work of the Ic section. The 03 sub-section's duties are set out in the organisation chart mentioned earlier. The sub-section's principal role was to analyse the 'enemy' situation and provide a coherent picture of the enemy's strength, location, activities and probable future intentions. This analysis took the form of a daily Feindlage—enemy situation report. Morning and Evening Reports were also produced daily. Each contained brief details of enemy activity during the period since the last report, expanding where appropriate on earlier reports.

The Feindlage was passed to the Ic (Lt. Col. Warnstorff) and discussed at the daily Ic morning conference, after which any re-drafting he required would be carried out before he then attended the daily Chief of Staff briefing, where he presented the report detailing the enemy situation.

The 03 sub-section's Feindlage was produced by collating and evaluating information received from a variety of sources. Of importance were the daily reports sent to the Army Group HQ by each subordinate division and corps within the area of Army Group E. These reports included the results of evaluation of any captured documents or prisoner interrogations. In addition the Army Group could draw on the results of aerial reconnaissance, the monitoring of enemy wireless networks and reports from agents and other sympathisers. In some cases prisoners were sent to Salonika or even to Germany for further interrogation, and material from these would be added to that received from the other sources.

The 03 sub-section was also responsible for the Tätigkeitsberichte—activity reports—usually produced monthly, which summarised the principal activities of the Ic section during the period. The AO section also produced an activity report, which is considered later when the subject of the degree of separation between the Ic and A0 sections is covered. Copies of these reports survive for the period July–September 1944. They provide valuable illustrations of the tasks of the Ic section and the components of its contribution to the overall work of the headquarters. (Annex 10).

* The numbering of Ordonnanz Offiziere was seemingly not standardised. The 05 in an Army Group corresponded to the 06 in an Army Headquarters.

The duties of the 03, as distinct from those of his sub-section, were the compilation of the morning and evening reports summarising the enemy situation and preparing such other reports as were required, including the monthly Ic 'activity' report.

As can be seen from the chart of duties within Ic/AO, one duty falling specifically to the 03 from 15 February 1944 (when the post of the 05 officer was abolished) was the maintenance of the confidential documents register (V. S. Brieftagebuch). This required the registering of incoming classified material with a short description of each item. It is probable that Lt. Waldheim's role was of a supervisory nature and that the actual task of entering these items fell to the clerks within the registry which, according to one of the clerks from the Ic section, consisted of a Corporal and a senior private (1). This registry also sorted the incoming post and distributed it as necessary. The role of such a registry in distribution is demonstrated by a contemporary document from Army Group F's files where the officer responsible for Allied forces has written on one piece received from Army Group E which concerned Allied forces: 'Osterbauer: why has this gone to the AO? In future I will get these things first'. (cf. p. 53 and Annex 77).

It is unclear if there was a separate classified register for AO material in the main registry or if the AO section kept this itself. AO material in Army Group F's headquarters was clearly given a different sequential number from the Ic/AO material (see Annex 221).

There has been some confusion over the significance of both the stamps on documents and the initialling of such stamps within the Ic/AO Branch. The standard branch stamp was headed 'Obkdo. H.Gr.E Ic/AO' and had boxes below for the initials of various post-holders (e.g. the Ic, 03, 05, AO). This allowed for a document's distribution by the registry to those and for its initialling by those to whom it was relevant. Clearly not every item that came into the general branch registry was relevant to and therefore went to the AO, although it was necessary that he, (as with the other post holders) should be included on the stamp. Given this and the role of the 03 as assistant to the Ic, it seems only normal that the O3 should have initialled much of the routine Ic material. However it would be unwise to draw any firm conclusions on the question of whether Lt. Waldheim saw pure AO material as well in this way, just on the basis of there being a space for the AO's initials on the standard stamp.

However, whatever the details of the registration of incoming material, Lt. Waldheim's duties included receiving written reports, telephone calls, etc that came into the Ic section generally rather than for any specific individual: this meant that the 03 was quite properly in a position to be well acquainted with the general picture on operations and the enemy response as perceived by the Germans and recorded in these sources.

Although Lt. Col. Warnstorff told the Austrian Commission that his 03 had been informed of virtually every event, Kurt Waldheim told the same body that he knew only a fraction of what Warnstorff knew. The 'Need to Know' order, issued by Hitler in January 1940, may well have restricted the knowledge of the 03 and the other junior officers. This order said that no-one, whether a post-holder or officer, was to be told of a 'classified' matter when it was not strictly necessary for the performance of his service duties. As the Austrian Commission noted, in May 1944 the Chief of Staff of Army Group E's Headquarters expressly referred to this order when amending the standard distribution lists within the headquarters (2).

Within the 03 sub-section there were a number of individuals responsible for specific tasks and for providing a specialist contribution to the section's work of evaluation. According to the 'Duties' chart, there were two other officers besides Lt. Waldheim—Oberleutnant Krohne (later replaced by Sonderführer Fischer) and Oberleutnant Poliza. They were respectively responsible for covering:

a. the situation in Greece and the Partisan areas; this also included Bulgaria, Serbia, Croatia, Montenegro and Albania.

b. the Allied situation in areas comprising Great Britain, the USA, France, Africa, Middle East; Foreign policy questions; and assessment of the results of the monitoring of the enemy radio network.

All the officers had the assistance of NCOs who were experts in relevant foreign languages and specific subjects such as the organisation and methods of particular enemy forces. Some of these men were civilians specifically employed on account of their particular qualifications (e.g. as interpreters, technicians, etc), and were called Sonderführer—this group contained several ranks, e.g.:

Sonderführer	G	equivalent	to	Senior Private
"	Z (Zug)	"	"	platoon commander
"	K (Kompanie)	"	"	company commander
"	B (Battaillon)	"	"	battalion commander
"	R (Regiment)	"	"	colonel

According to an NCO in the Ic section from 1943–45, Lt. Poliza for example had a Sonderführer G who was an English interpreter/translator who worked in conjunction with an Army NCO.

These two 03 sub-section officers also had administrative duties. For example Lt. Krohne was generally responsible for Sonderaufgaben—special tasks such as escorting visiting senior officers, acting as a courier (not to be confused with the term Sonderbehandlung used in connection with the 'Commando Order'). Lt. Poliza was responsible for personnel matters i.e. administrative matters relating to individual members of the Ic/AO Branch.

As the chart shows, Lts. Krohne and Poliza were responsible for Gefangenenvernehmung, the interrogation of prisoners. Such interrogation was usually confined to those prisoners of particular interest to the Army Group and to each of the officer's respective areas of interest. This subject is covered more fully later.

Powers of the 03

Kurt Waldheim held only a fairly junior rank equivalent to a Lieutenant (Lt) in the British Army. He, like Lt. Poliza, was not a Regular soldier and was not a member of the General Staff Corps. It has already been noted that the 03 was not the Deputy to the Ic: this was the AO, Maj. Hammer. If for some reason both the Ic and AO were absent, any important questions would be passed for a decision to the Operations officer (the Ia) who, like the Ic, was a General Staff Officer and who was the nominated stand-in in such circumstances.

Although Lt. Waldheim was the assistant to the Ic, according to Lt. Poliza, he was only 'Primus inter Pares' i.e. first among equals. He possessed no formal authority over Lt. Poliza and Lt. Krohne but, although they were not technically subordinate they acted as his assistants. Lt. Poliza believed that the only people over whom Lt. Waldheim could really exercise any de facto control were the men in the office (3). Lt. Col. Warnstorff in his affidavit of 15 June 1987 (4) stated that the only 'assignment' of the 03 was to inform the 'members of the lower staff' (cartographers, translators, drivers etc) about the enemy situation. One of the specialist NCOs, Wende, has stated that Lt. Waldheim did not have the authority himself to order his actions; such orders would come from the Ic (5). Poliza has added that Lt. Waldheim most definitely did not possess any 'command authority': this term refers to the power to give orders, usually of an operational nature, to field troops. This last point was endorsed by Lt. Col. Warnstorff in his affidavit. No evidence has been found to contradict this.

The testimony of his colleagues and other German staff officers is that Lt. Waldheim's primary role as the 03 was to act as the collator of the material submitted by his colleagues covering their specialist areas, and to compile the synopsis of the important points, perhaps reducing the material to 20% of the original whole. There have even been suggestions that he was not himself an expert in any particular field but a good evaluator and presenter of the data (6). In order to fulfil this task he would naturally have been expected to achieve a good grasp of the overall enemy situation and to have the ability to identify important developments and relate seemingly disparate events to provide a guide to likely future developments. He may have prepared special analyses of future enemy intentions if required, again based largely on input from his specialist colleagues. However, during the period concerning this Review, in addition to his normal leave, and some weeks of sick leave, Waldheim was also granted extra leave to continue his academic studies. When he was absent his duties fell to Lt. Poliza and Lt. Krohne. These sometimes fairly lengthy absences amounting to some three and a half months in one nine month period (see chronology) would suggest that he was just one of a team and not an indispensable expert.

During any of the briefings of senior officers which the 03 may have been ordered to attend, his task would have been to assist Lt. Col. Warnstorff, the Ic, in presenting the report of the enemy situation and to answer any detailed points raised. From the albeit few surviving contemporary documents, both Lt. Waldheim and other junior officers on occasion did present prepared papers on specific points at these meetings (Annex 11). If Lt. Waldheim was absent on leave another officer from the 03 sub-section would present any paper required. (Annex 12).

Such records of the actual discussions at these briefings as have survived reveal no participation in the meetings by Lt. Waldheim beyond the presentation of prepared papers on specific subjects, but the records are only a summary of key points. His predecessor as O3 (Lt. Schollen) has stated that it is very unlikely that Lt. Waldheim often made proposals or suggestions at such briefings, as he would not have expected Kurt Waldheim to attend them on a regular basis (7). The suggestion that the 03 could direct operational deployments or make proposals has been dismissed by Lt. Poliza who said 'all such matters were outside our competence and function' (8). While Lt. Schollen said 'he answered questions and so on' (9). Lt. Müller-Mangeot the 01 from Rhodes has recently stated that the Wehrmacht was rather strict in its differentiation between different functions and tasks. It was not, he claims, considered appropriate for a junior officer such as an Ordonnanz Offiziere to do more than provide information about his particular field of responsibility (10). Further when Lt. Col. Warnstorff was asked by the Austrian Commission if Waldheim made suggestions or comments during such meetings, Warnstorff emphatically denied this, saying that Waldheim's job was to help him with the enemy situation report; he would have been swiftly 'reminded of' his role by Warnstorff if he had tried to go beyond that. (11).

Co-operation between Intelligence and Counter-Intelligence Sections

The method of working within the Ic/AO Branch—especially how, and how far the AO section and the Ic section co-operated and were aware of each other's work, particularly in terms of the AO's involvement with other Intelligence or security bodies such as the SD—is an important aspect.

There was a clear distinction between 'intelligence officers' (i.e. those personnel who were trained in intelligence matters and operated in that field all the time, whether in an Army unit or Headquarters, or with one of the intelligence agencies) and those Army or other Service personnel who were posted to a unit or Headquarters to carry out a staff job which involved the collation and assessment of intelligence but who would usually leave that post and return to other Service duties. This distinction is common to many armies and the examination of contemporary material on the German professional intelligence organisation—the Abwehr—demonstrates it clearly.

Although the Ic of the Army Group had authority over all counter-intelligence units operating in his area, and his duties included liaison with the SS, SD and GFP, this authority was exercised through the AO, who was the professional intelligence representative within the Army Group HQ. The duties of the AO concerned counter-intelligence, co-ordination and control of counter-intelligence troops and the GFP, and liaison with other intelligence and security agencies, notably the Abwehr and the SD. In the case of the SD this involvement increased to an even greater degree in the summer of 1944 once the SD replaced the Abwehr as the main intelligence organisation, effectively absorbing it.

Allied wartime and early post-war research confirms that counter-intelligence matters were the responsibility of the AO who in some cases communicated directly with the Foreign Counter-Intelligence Office of the OKW or, following the Abwehr's demise, with the Reich Central Security Headquarters (RSHA). From these bodies he also received some direct instructions for his counter-intelligence work. An AO it seems often enjoyed some measure of independence in at least some aspects of his work, the extent varying from headquarters to headquarters and between individual Ics and AOs.

The Army Group Headquarters had at its disposal within the Army Group a number of units consisting of professional intelligence personnel. Most of these were organised in counter-intelligence bodies called Abwehrkommando, with subordinate Abwehrtrupp. The latter established where necessary smaller Meldenkopf, which were in fact just small reporting stations, at corps or divisional level. With the demise of the Abwehr these were retitled and the Abwehr prefix was replaced by Frontaufklärung (Front reconnaissance) giving the abbreviations FAK and FAT sometimes seen on documents from the Ic/AO Branch. The numbering of these units reflected their parent department (Amt). Within the Abwehr those with numbers in the 100 series were from Amt I and dealt with operational intelligence; the 200s came from Amt II and dealt with sabotage and subversion while the 300s and Amt III concentrated on counter-intelligence and security.

The work of the AO section is illustrated by the monthly 'Activity Reports' from one of which the following extract is taken (Annex 13).

September 1944

Orders [to all units] up to divisional level to destroy all records relating to Allied Military Missions and members of 'commando' units.

....

Orders for the creation of false soldier's identity books for GFP personnel.

....

Deputizing for Lt. Col. Warnstorff in his absence [14–27]

....

Orders to Front Reconnaissance Troop (FAT) 250 to blow up the Struma bridges.

....

Instructions to XXII(Mtn) Corps on the deception of the enemy on the direction of our withdrawal.

....

Announcement of Maj. Manowski's succession to Maj. Grün (SD Salonika) [19.9].

....

This work can be contrasted with the reports for the Ic section's activities for the same period:

September 1944

Preparation of the Ic Daily Reports on the basis of the reports from subordinate commands and Front Reconnaissance units (FATs).

....

Analysis of the latest data on enemy situation and up-dating of the card index and situation maps.

....

Evaluation of captured documents, prisoner of war interrogation reports and intercepted enemy signals traffic.

....

Preparation of briefing for the Chief of Staff conferences and for the weekly situation report.

....

Preparation of situation maps for the fronts in France, Italy, Russia and the Far East.

....

Evaluation of the reports on enemy sea and air operations from the Army, Navy and Air Force, including the evaluation of aerial reconnaissance received from the Air Liaison officer (Ic.L) in conjunction with the Air Force in Greece and the South East.

From the contemporary documents and details of duties, it is evident that a distinction was made between the field of work of the Ic and AO sections. However it is not possible now to be certain about the precise degree of working contact which existed in Army Group E's Headquarters between the AO section and the remainder of the Ic/AO Branch. Apart from the physical separation of the sections—according to Lt. Poliza the AO section was in another building on the other side of the road—(12) it has been suggested that the 'Need to Know' order issued by Hitler in January 1940 would have restricted the more junior Ic section officers' knowledge of AO matters, but how far this was actually true in practice is unclear.

When asked by the Austrian Commission about the relationship between the Ic and the AO sections, Lt. Col. Warnstorff, the Ic and Head of the whole Group, said that he never discussed the technical details of the counter-intelligence side even with his AO. He considered that there was a clear cut distinction between the work of the Ic and the AO. Warnstorff emphasised that in his view this distinction was far clearer than was the case in some other headquarters such as that of the German 14 Army in Italy, examples of whose Ic/AO Branch's workings were mentioned by the Austrian Commission during their discussion with him. He gave the impression that the AO carried on his work very much in isolaton from the rest of the Group. Warnstorff stated for example, that he personally did not speak with the SD or the SS in Salonika, and that any such dealings must therefore have fallen to Maj. Hammer the AO (13). This view of complete separation of Ic and AO work was supported by the testimony of other members of the Ic Section. For example Lt. Schollen (Lt. Waldheim's predecessor as 03) stated during the Thames Television interviews that, although Maj. Hammer sometimes spoke to him about what he did, this was only in very general terms. He did not work with him and their areas of activity were quite separate (14).

On the other hand it has been suggested by Maj. Lützow, who was an assistant to the Ia—the operations officer—of the Army Group E headquarters' staff in December 1944 and January 1945, that AO affairs were not kept separate from the rest of the Branch and that the Ic staff would not only have been aware of AO work but may also have been actively involved in it. He claims that, as the task of the Ic section was to locate the major concentrations of enemy forces, including partisans, while the AO would try and establish through his agents the identities, sources of supply etc. of the partisans, their work was closely interlinked (15).

Cpl. Mayer, who served in the Personnel Section of the Army Group E Headquarters, made allegations (whilst a prisoner of war in Yugoslavian hands in 1947) concerning Lt. Waldheim. Mayer's testimony related to events in Yugoslavia, not involving British servicemen. The only point of relevance to this Review is Mayer's claim that Lt. Waldheim had both a role as an 'espionage officer' and also close involvement with other counter-intelligence activities carried out by the SD. However there is no other verbal or documentary evidence to support his claims which, some have suggested, were given to satisfy his captors and which were included in the Yugoslav case (Annex 14).

It seems probable that the position of the head of the Ic/AO Branch (Lt. Col. Warnstorff) in relation to the AO will have been different from that of the other members of the Ic section. In order to conform to the dictates of security, and Hitler's 'Need to Know' order, it will probably have been the norm to avoid letting persons outside the AO section know the more sensitive details of the Section's work; but the Ic had obviously to be kept in the picture. Indeed, contemporary documents indicate that the Ic was more fully informed of the work of the AO than has sometimes been suggested and that he participated in discussions and decisions about at least some aspects of it.

For example the Ic 'Activity Report' for September 1944 shows that the Ic went to Athens to discuss counter-intelligence matters. The text also mentions 'R-netz' which, as is known from other material, was the espionage and sabotage network being set up by the German intelligence agencies to operate after the impending German withdrawal. A German Abwehr officer who served in Greece at that time gave evidence that he had dealt not only with Maj. Hammer but also with Lt. Col. Warnstorff who had been informed of his activities (cf. p. 103).

Although the other Ic section officers, especially those of the 03 sub-section, claim they knew little of the work of the AO section, they must clearly have received information from the AO where this was relevant to their areas of responsibility. It might seem odd that one of the specialist NCOs suggested that he had no contact with the GFP or Abwehr, since one of his tasks was to build up the picture of Greek partisan activity and he will have relied heavily on information from these sources. It is possible however that such information was passed to him through intermediaries without any direct contact.

It would seem unwise, however, to conclude that a complete separation existed between the sections with the effect that no-one outside the AO section knew anything at all about its work or its outside contacts. The officer from the Abwehr mentioned above knew several of the Army Group's junior Ic staff by name including Lts. Waldheim and Poliza. Further, the testimony in 1947 of an NCO of the Ic section (Annex 9) suggests that various counter-intelligence and GFP personnel attended the Ic meeting where they will have met some of the staff of the Ic section. Clearly the subordinate officers of the 03 sub-section will also have needed to know some information from the AO domain for their own duties. But it is not unreasonable to suppose that the details of the work of the AO section (including its communications with the units under its control and the other agencies) were not common knowledge to members of the Ic section.

The interrogation of prisoners of war

In common with all armies, the German Army recognised that prisoners of war often provided a valuable source of intelligence on a variety of subjects. The interrogation of prisoners was standard practice and was legal under the International Laws of Warfare provided that the methods used did not breach the provisions of the 1929 Geneva Convention governing the treatment of prisoners of war.

Allied servicemen captured by the Germans usually received only a standard initial and somewhat perfunctory interrogation before being passed into the routine administrative machinery to move them to a prisoner of war camp. However, in the Balkans in 1943-44, as a consequence of the German anxiety to obtain an insight into Allied plans with regard to the theatre, captured Allied servicemen who might have especial knowledge of Allied plans or important operations or units were interrogated more thoroughly and by a higher level of command than usual.

To German eyes 'commandos' and members of the Allied Military Missions were just such individuals. For this reason Army Group F ordered in April 1944 through Army Group E that, as far as possible, 'commandos' were to be taken prisoner and, after preliminary interrogation at divisional or corps level, should be passed to Army Group E headquarters for further interrogation.

The categorisation of any Allied servicemen who were captured rested primarily with the intelligence officers of the force making the initial capture. In the Balkans as elsewhere an important factor in deciding the correct category for a prisoner was the circumstances in which he had been captured. For example, Allied personnel captured during the large scale conventional fighting on the Dodecanese Islands in late 1943 were usually considered to be 'ordinary' soldiers even when their unit formed part of the Allies' Special Forces, as in the case of the Long Range Desert Group. These men were quite quickly passed through the normal prisoner of war administrative chain to camps in Germany (cf. Chap 10. Sec. a) However, those personnel captured on 'special operations' or in circumstances where large scale operations were not in progress would usually be regarded as 'commandos'. Nevertheless the prisoner's category could, it seems, be amended as a result of information obtained at a later date, as one of the cases examined later demonstrates (cf. p. 42 and Annex 58).

Although the interrogation of those Allied prisoners of war who were sent to the Army Group Headquarters at Salonika was the responsibility of the 03 sub-section and specifically that of the two officers Lt. Poliza and Lt. Krohne, all the contemporary evidence points to such prisoners being detained and questioned in prisons in the town itself and not in the Headquarters complex at Arsakli. This is supported by the recent statements of Ic staff (16).

Lt. Poliza has said he and Lt. Krohne would decide the line of questioning and the areas of especial relevance to their respective spheres of interest and the prisoner's origins. Once agreed, the requirements would be passed to Krohne's and Poliza's subordinate interpreters and specialists: the latter apparently usually carried out the actual interrogations, although Poliza has recently said that he did on occasion attend the interrogations himself (17). The then Cpl. Wollschläger, a good English speaker and one of the specialist interpreters, has recently stated that he was usually told by Lt. Poliza or Cpl. Wende the areas of especial interest but that he normally interrogated prisoners alone (18). The incident recently mentioned by the then Cpl. Wende, the specialist in Greek matters subordinate to Lt. Krohne—in which he accompanied Cpl. H Wollschläger when the latter interrogated two Allied officers who had been captured with the partisans (and who were therefore of particular interest to Wende)—was apparently an exception (19).

As distinct from this later testimony, there is little contemporary evidence on the extent of the direct involvement of personnel from the Ic section in the interrogation of prisoners in Salonika. Surviving Allied personnel who were interrogated there by the Army Group or others made no positive identifications of any Ic individuals when debriefed on liberation at the end of the war. However the accounts of two British officers, one concerning Salonika and one later in Mitrovica, do make references to an individual who is probably Lt. Col. Warnstorff (cf. p. 87 and 89).

The information gained from such interrogations was collated by the appropriate officer and passed to the 03 who would consider it in the context of other relevant information. He would then submit to the Ic either the interrogating officer's assessment with just a covering letter of his own, or only his own assessment of the information gained from the interrogation supplemented by that from other sources. The resultant assessment was passed up the Ic chain to Army Group F and where appropriate to the OKH and OKW.

Lt. Waldheim would have been aware of the arrival of prisoners in Salonika for interrogation and he would have known that interrogations were taking place. Further, he may have been involved in some of the discussions concerning areas or topics of particular interest that should be covered during interrogations. However he has consistently and strongly denied any personal involvement in the actual interrogation of prisoners of war (20). This claim is supported both by the testimony of his colleagues, several of whom have however said that they themselves did carry out interrogations, and also by his predecessor (Lt. Schollen) who similarly denies having conducted any interrogations during his service as 03 at Arsakli (21). Certainly, the liberation debriefs of surviving Allied servicemen who were interrogated in Salonika include no indentifications that can be related to Lt. Waldheim by name or position either as one of the interrogators or as being present during interrogations.

Although the testimony of surviving German servicemen is that their interrogation methods were quite proper, the accounts of surviving 'commandos' indicate some less than correct treatment while in prison. These cases are considered later: in general the allegations by ex-prisoners of ill-treatment were laid not against men of the Army Group Headquarters' staff but against the prison staff from the Geheime Feldpolizei (GFP)—the Secret Field Police—which is discussed next.

The Geheime Feldpolizei

The GFP was an Army not an SS or police body, although many of its members came from the police, especially the Security Police (SIPO), and had close links with these other organisations. Although the GFP was not a part of the Army Group Headquarters itself, there were GFP units under the latter's command and they played an important part in the matters under review. The tasks of the GFP as laid down in its Field Manual were:

a. The prevention and discovery of sabotage and other offences against security in the German Armed Forces as well as of all other military or civilian tendencies and actions within the zone of operations which might be hostile to the Nazi State.

b. The execution of all security measures within forward and rear zones of operation.

c. The identification and registration of persons suitable to act as agents.

d. The execution of all Security Police tasks not within the field of action of the Feldgendarmerie (the ordinary Military Police).

e. The briefing of all military headquarters and the issuing of directives on questions affecting military security.

f. All other functions of military intelligence in co-operation with, and according to instructions from the Headquarters.

Special emphasis was placed on the prevention of sabotage, demoralising propaganda and rumour-mongering. This work included the control of identity papers, travel permits and supervision of all civilian movement in forward and rear areas. Measures to prevent civilians joining in any action against the occupying forces were especially important.

These duties involved the GFP in the collection of information about actual and potential enemies, particularly partisans. According to an ex-member of the GFP in Salonika, there was a two-way flow of information between the Ic/AO Group and GFP, the latter especially using its contacts within the civilian population to verify and expand on reports from other sources. In order to ensure a proper flow of information between the Ic/AO Branch and the GFP, a liaison officer from the latter (in this case an NCO) was attached to the Ic/AO Branch at Arsakli from the autumn of 1943. More senior GFP personnel also visited Arsakli and attended meetings there as necessary, if possible, weekly (22).

As the Army Group E staff duties table shows, responsibility for the control and deployment of the GFP rested with the AO under the general direction of the Ic. However the GFP also had its own internal hierarchy responsible for the day to day administration of the units: at its head was a Field Police Commissioner who for most of the period in question was Commander Alois Uch.

Of especial importance to this Review are the GFP's duties in running at least one prison and a prison camp within Salonika and their conduct of interrogations there. The inmates of the prisons were usually civilians thought to be 'hostile' and any German Service personnel considered to be security risks or involved in illegal activities such as black-market selling of weapons and munitions. The 'hostile' category covered those individuals believed to be engaged in, or sympathetic to, the partisan activities which were of great interest to the counter-intelligence organisations (as well as to the ordinary military authorities). Given the official German view of Allied servicemen who had been captured either during 'commando' raids or whilst helping the partisans, their detention by the GFP was to be expected, especially as the 'Commando Order' strictly forbade the placement of 'commandos' in standard prisoner of war camps. (The 'Commando Order' is discussed in detail in Chapter 5).

The NCO from the GFP who acted as the liaison officer with the Ic/AO Branch at Army Group E's Headquarters has recently said that he knew that there were some beatings and irregularities during interrogations at the GFP prison. However he claimed that these were not standard practice (23). As already mentioned, the Ic had some responsibility and authority over the GFP, exercised usually through his AO. One contemporary document, the AO 'Activity' report for August 1944 (Annex 12), mentions a visit by Lt. Col. Warnstorff and Maj. Hammer to the GFP prison. However it is still unclear how far Warnstorff's direct control extended to the GFP treatment of prisoners in their hands. There is, however, no evidence that Lt. Waldheim had any responsibility for the GFP or its activities or had any control over these.

Responsibility within the Ic/AO Branch for the transfer of Allied prisoners from Army Control

There is only limited surviving evidence available on the procedures governing the handling of Allied servicemen brought specially to Salonika for interrogation. However it appears that Lt. Col. Warnstorff on at least one occasion personally met a party of prisoners—probably in cases where they were of especial importance or interest (cf. p. 49)—and that other officers could be used briefly to act as escorts. This role has been stated by a British officer to have been carried out on one occasion by Lt. Waldheim (cf. p. 80).

Surviving German documents record another incident involving the movement of British prisoners of war in which Lt. Waldheim briefly played a part. This case, which is examined more fully later (cf. p. 79), concerned British servicemen who were both regarded and treated by the Germans as ordinary prisoners of war and not as 'commandos'. The documents show that Lt. Waldheim acted briefly as a channel for the passage of information and orders concerning the incident. The subsequent handling of the matter and the men's transfer to a standard prisoner of war camp were conducted through the normal channels: the men were not taken to Salonika for interrogation.

It is impossible to determine with any great certainty the degree of routine involvement of the Ic section and O3 sub-section in prisoner of war handling and administration.

On the specific issue of the removal of 'commando' prisoners from the jurisdiction of Army Group E's Headquarters and their transfer to the SD, there is again only limited surviving evidence. In the case of the Alimnia 'commandos' (see Chapter 7) the signal requesting a decision on their disposal was classified 'Geheime Kommandosache' (abbreviated to gKdos)*. The contemporary German Staff manual states that any officer, and senior NCO who had been so authorised, could handle and issue signals bearing this classification (Annex 15). It has been claimed however by Lt. Poliza of the Ic section—in the Thames Television programme—that only the Ic (Lt. Col. Warnstorff) and his deputy (Maj. Hammer the AO) could authorise and hence initiate the despatch of signals bearing this classification. This implies that the responsibility for the despatch of such signals rested with them. Lt. Col. Warnstorff too stated that he believed that Maj. Hammer must have sent this signal (25).

The reply to the above signal shows only that the order for the men's release to the SD came from the Ic/AO Branch of F to the Ic/AO Branch of E. On the evidence available and according to the surviving officers' testimony both to the Austrian Commission and to the Thames Television programme, the correct procedure would be for such orders to be passed to the AO by the Ic and for appropriate further orders to be given by the AO (26) (or perhaps, his deputy, Sonderführer Schlenker) to the GFP in whose hands the prisoners almost certainly were.

Not only does this process, whereby the responsibility for such transfers fell to the AO Maj. Hammer, now deceased, conform to the collective testimony of the surviving Ic members but it also fits with the duties shown as falling to the AO section. Among the duties listed for the AO's deputy (Sonderführer Schlenker) in the aforementioned chart is 'Aufgaben auf dem Kgf. Gebiet'—tasks relating to prisoner of war matters. Although this was no doubt mainly concerned with security aspects of prisoner of war camps etc., his role confirms the AO section's involvement in the prisoner of war field and, in the light of the AO's responsibility for the day to day work of the GFP and his liaison with the SD, this section's control of such transfers is not unlikely.

Further, the system, as set out in the discussions at the OKW when the 'Commando Order' was initiated, laid down that the transfer of any 'commandos' to the SD was to take place through the counter-intelligence channel (Annex 16).

Among the few papers of the GFP units which have survived, are some from Army Group F which provide monthly figures for arrests, executions etc. These also include figures for transfers to the SD, clearly a routine matter for the GFP (Annex 17).

CHAPTER 4: References

(1) Documentation produced by the Austrian Ministry of Foreign Affairs: 'The White Book'. Statement by R. Voigt. (Subsequently called White Book).

* This means 'Secret Command Matter'. According to British research this is the equivalent of UK Secret rather than Top Secret: the latter was the initial wartime and early postwar American interpretation (24).

(2) Report of the Austrian Commission of Historians: interview with Lt. Col. Warnstorff. (Subsequently called Austrian Commission).

(3) Thames Television. Testimony for the programme 'Waldheim: a Case to Answer?' (Subsequently called Thames Television).

(4) White Book.

(5) Thames Television.

(6) Thames Television.

(7) Thames Television.

(8) Thames Television: unbroadcast statement.

(9) Thames Television: unbroadcast statement.

(10) Thames Television: unbroadcast statement.

(11) Austrian Commission.

(12) Thames Television.

(13) Austrian Commission.

(14) Thames Television.

(15) Thames Television: unbroadcast statement.

(16) Austrian Commission and correspondence with Ministry of Defence (MOD).

(17) Thames Television.

(18) Correspondence with MOD.

(19) Thames Television and correspondence with MOD.

(20) White Book.

(21) Thames Television: unbroadcast statement.

(22) Thames Television: unbroadcast statement.

(23) Thames Television.

(24) MOD Archives.

(25) Austrian Commission.

(26) Austrian Commission and Thames Television.

A set of the Thames Television material cited in this report has been deposited by Thames Television with the Wiener Library, in London.

Chapter 5: The 'Commando Order' and the German attitude to prisoners

Background

The cases of British servicemen which have been raised with the Ministry of Defence concern for the most part members of the Special Forces.

Their treatment if captured or encountered by the Germans was inextricably linked with the German attitude to the form of warfare typified by the 'commando' raids of the years 1940–42. As this had a direct effect on their fate, this section considers Hitler's so-called 'Commando Order' of October 1942 in some detail and, in particular, seeks to shed light on how it was understood and applied by the German forces at the time.

From 1940 Britain initiated a policy of amphibious and airborne raids on German occupied territory intended to cause 'alarm and despondency' in the enemy's ranks, to tie down his forces in defensive duties against such raids, and to gather intelligence for possible future operations. The raids took place from North Norway to the Bay of Biscay and throughout the Mediterranean.

In response to this British strategy, a Führerbefehl (i.e. an order made on the personal and direct authority of Hitler as Supreme Commander of the German Armed Forces)—one of many such orders effected during the course of the war—was issued in October 1942. It said that members of such raiding parties should in effect be killed as spies or saboteurs: this denied them the protection both of the Hague Laws of War covering the right to surrender at discretion, and of the Geneva Convention covering their treatment once surrendered or if captured.

The order is known by different titles. The Allies have traditionally called it the 'Commando Order' which is the term used in this Review. In contemporary German usage it was the 'Führerbefehl of 18 October 1942' or the order of the same date relating to the treatment of 'sabotage' or 'commando troops'.

What the Order said

The order (text at Annex 18) essentially laid down two rules:

Enemy personnel engaged in 'so-called commando operations', even if in uniform and whether armed or not, were to be eliminated in combat down to the last man. Any attempts by such individuals to surrender were to be rejected and the men killed.

Where such 'commandos' acting as 'Agents, Saboteurs, etc.' fell into the hands of the Wehrmacht indirectly, e.g. from the Police in the occupied countries, they were to be handed over to the SD immediately. In no instance were such individuals to be held in military custody, for example, in prisoner of war (PW) camps.

The role of the SD in such cases was not explained. Presumably the implications required no clarification, or specific instructions may have been passed to that organisation by another channel. The order excluded from these provisions enemy soldiers engaged in normal (i.e. large scale) military operations, including those captured at sea or aircrew who bailed-out from their aircraft.

While the order was classified 'secret', all commanders and officers had a duty to ensure that troops were aware of its requirements. Failure to do so or any obstruction of its execution was punishable by Court-Martial. An accompanying secret letter (text and translation at Annex 19) was issued on a more limited circulation to senior officers. This explained the background to the order in greater detail. In a significant addition to the order, the letter authorised interrogation where expedient in exceptional circumstances prior to execution viz: 'should the occasion arise for the purposes of interrogation where it is considered necessary to spare one or two men, as soon as their interrogation is complete they are to be shot.' The letter did not identify who was to be responsible for either interrogation or execution and there was no reference in it to the SD.

The covering letter also placed in the 'commando' category any Allied personnel who landed from boats or submarines or parachuted down to help indigenous resistance forces to carry out 'sabotage'.

When examining contemporary documents confusion can arise if it is not appreciated that, whereas some officers clearly saw the letter as an integral part of the Führerbefehl and referred to it as such, nevertheless its circulation was so restricted and its terms so little known that others apparently did not recognise that reference to the Order might cover the letter as well as the Führerbefehl itself (Annex 20).

Reasons for the Order

According to Gen. Warlimont of OKW, an officer closely involved in the drafting of the order, the key events leading to its issue appear to have been the Allied Combined Operation against Dieppe in August 1942 and 'commando' raids in Norway. In the German view, the methods employed in such operations were in breach of the laws of war, particularly in respect of the treatment of Germans taken prisoner during the course of the Allied operations.

The OKW's Foreign Department summary of such acts claimed that the British operation order for the raid on Dieppe stated that wherever possible the Allied troops should tie the hands of prisoners to prevent them destroying their documents. It continued:

> In accordance with this order, in the course of the raid on DIEPPE, Cpl. Kurt MÜLLER (7 Inf. Regt 571) and several wounded German soldiers had their hands or their thumbs tied behind their backs whilst they lay on the ground. In the same way, several men attached to the TODT Organisation were bound. In one case, the cords were placed round his (the victim's) neck and pulled down his back to his thumbs which were tied together, so that he was in danger of choking when he allowed his arms to drop owing to fatigue. . . .

> These numerous cases go to prove that those concerned, chiefly members of Canadian troops, had been systematically trained in this kind of binding which is contrary to international law (Cpt. FAIRBAIR'S system All-in Fighting) and were also correspondingly equipped.

Their account of a 'commando' operation in Norway stated:

> On the 16.9.1942 10 English and 2 Norwegians in the uniform of the British mountain rifle regiment . . . . heavily armed and equipped with explosives of every description, landed on the Norwegian coast. They blew up important plant of the Glomfjord power station at midnight on the 21.9. A German sentinel was shot in the process. The Norwegian workers were threatened that they would be chloroformed, should they offer resistance. The British had brought hypodermic syringes along with them for the purpose (1).

In this latter case the carriage of drugs for use in such operations was seen as an illegal method of warfare.

However, the discussions within the OKW and the explanatory letter that accompanied the text of the actual 'Commando Order' indicate that, apart from a belief that the proposed treatment of such raiders was appropriate in the light of their own illegal acts, a major factor in the German decision to issue this order, perhaps the most important, was the danger that such Allied raids posed to the German war economy.

How the Order was disseminated

The essentials of the Führerbefehl were announced to the world in the public Wehrmachtbericht (Armed Forces Report) broadcast by German radio on 7 October 1942 (Annex 21). But, as already mentioned, the internal notification to the German Forces of the policy was by top secret letter on a limited distribution and not for retention below brigade level. Indeed, not long afterwards, instructions were issued for the withdrawal of copies of the order from the lowest levels of command and for their destruction to be notified to the OKW by the appropriate Army level headquarters.

Therefore, although the text itself was not widely circulated, which helps to explain the claims of some German officers and servicemen that they had never seen a copy and were in consequence unaware of how it was worded, there was widespread knowledge of its key provisions and general tenor, disseminated probably verbally or in a paraphrased form as the Order itself instructed. This also accounts for references to its basic principles in German Army documents of the period.

Although prepared to broadcast that 'commandos' had been eliminated in combat, the Germans were unwilling to admit publicly to executions after capture. They then went to great lengths, seemingly, to see that copies of the order did not fall into enemy hands and later, that all relevant papers were destroyed. A reflection of this policy was the later instruction sent out by Army Group E in September 1944, just before the German withdrawal from Greece directing the destruction of all 'commando'-related papers held from division level downwards (cf Annex 13, September report). In the event some higher level formations including Army Group E itself, appear also to have destroyed such papers.

German application of the 'Commando Order'

General

The 'Commando Order' was implemented by German forces in most theatres from 1942 onwards. Apart from the initial applications in Norway in 1942, there were also instances in France in 1942 and in Italy in 1943. Further, in spite of Allied protests made in 1943 (cf. p. 36), the OKW reminded its forces of the 'Commando Order' and clarified its application with regard to the new battle front following the successful Allied landings in Normandy in June 1944. They ordered that only those enemy troops fighting in uniform in the immediate battle front were if captured to be treated as prisoners of war. Enemy soldiers, especially paratroops, met outside this area were to be regarded as 'sabotage and terror' troops and dealt with accordingly (Annex 22). Probably because of the widespread use of large scale paratroop forces in the Normandy battle, this order provided clearer guidance about the 'accepted' limits of the immediate battle-zone (Annex 23). The OKW apparently believed (or wished to believe) that their earlier policy had worked and that 'commando' raids of the 1942 type had been reduced as a consequence of their 'firm' action, and that similar measures in Normandy would be as efficacious.

Under this new ruling, Allied troops (mainly members of the SAS) who clearly formed part of the Allied forces now firmly established in northern France were considered by the Germans to be 'saboteurs' because their role was to operate in the Germans' rear and to carry out harrassing operations either on their own or in conjunction with the forces of the French Resistance movement. As a result of the order, a considerable number of SAS soldiers so engaged were executed when captured.

However, surviving OKW papers suggest that there was not in fact one clear view as to how and when the 'Commando Order' should be applied and who did or did not fall within its provisions. Only some Allied soldiers captured on 'commando' operations, as so perceived by the Germans, were executed. In the North African theatre where Rommel was in command, the Order was not applied at all, although there were a large number of British operations that clearly fell into the category of 'commando' raids.

What is evident, however, is that within the OKW there was considerable interest in the activities of Allied 'commandos' and in the implementation of the 'Commando Order'.

In the Balkans

In 1942 when disseminating the 'Commando Order' Gen. Löhr—the Army Commander South-East, who later commanded Army Group E and held that post until the end of the war, being Lt. Waldheim's Commanding General for the period covered by this Review—added a postcript to the 'Commando Order' in which he said:

> I expect every superior officer to apply himself totally to seeing that the forces execute this order with brutal severity and without exception. I shall have every contravention investigated and those responsible mercilessly called to account (Annex 24).

At this time, however, the German forces in the Balkans were not greatly at risk from Allied 'commando' activities as the bulk of the Aegean islands were in Italian hands. Nevertheless the 'gist' of the 'Commando Order' was reflected in contemporary unit records. For example, in January 1943 the German Infantry Division on Crete recorded in its War Diary that:

> increased activity by British Commandos and Paratroop units are to be expected shortly . . . . they have to be destroyed ruthlessly according to the orders issued (Annex 25).

And an internal OKW letter written in May 1943 on the subject of 'sabotage troops' mentioned that a group of British service personnel captured south of Athens with a clandestine radio station would be treated as saboteurs (Annex 26 & cf. p. 93).

Following the Italian surrender, the re-deployment of German forces southwards to occupy territory previously held by Italian forces increased the likelihood of contact with 'commando' units. The growing German fear of an Allied landing in the Balkans, not really alleviated by the Allies' unsuccessful efforts in the Dodecanese islands at the end of 1943, was reflected in a growing number of references in German records to 'commandos' and their treatment.

In October 1943, in the area under command of 2 Panzer Army, 114 Jaeger Division part of XV Mountain Corps recorded in a 'Memorandum concerning Commando Operations' that:

> In order to prepare major landings, to support band [partisan] warfare and to perform all kinds of sabotage, the enemy conducts so-called commando operations . . . . [our] mission is always the complete destruction of the troops who have landed or were dropped by parachute, who deserve no consideration on account of their fighting methods, which are contrary to International Law (Annex 27).

According to a German deserter questioned in 1944, Army Group F ordered that all British agents or sabotage groups were to be 'destroyed immediately' (Annex 28).

Probably to clarify his own understanding of the 'Commando Order' in January 1944, the Senior Intelligence Officer in Army Group E (Lt. Col. Warnstorff—who has not long taken over from Lt. Col. von Harling who had become the Ic at Army Group F) asked the OKW for a copy of the original 'Commando Order'. In so doing he referred to the instructions relating to the 'handling of commandos', but the OKW in sending the text referred to the order on the 'handling of sabotage troops'. It is unclear whether the OKW also sent a copy of the supporting letter: on balance it would appear that they did not (Annex 29).

The interest at the OKW in 'commando' operations and the application of the 'Commando Order' in the Balkan area is demonstrated by events in early 1944. According to testimony in 1947 before an American Military Tribunal concerned with the 'Commando Order' and the OKW's role, when the 'commando' raids on Patmos and Piskopi on 19 and 23 February respectively came to Hitler's notice, the OKW sent a signal to the Commander-in-Chief South-East at Army Group F reminding him of the 'Commando Order' (2):

> Reference: Führer Order No 00383/42 g.K./OKW/WFSt of 18 October 1942.
>
> Re: Landing of British commandos on 19 and 23 February on the Dodecanese islands Patmos and Piskopi.
>
> In connection with the reported landings of British commandos on Patmos on 19 February and on Piskopi on 23 February, attention is again drawn to the relevant order (Annex 30).

In fact on neither of these occasions were any 'commandos' taken prisoner.

The special OKW files relating to 'commando' matters are incomplete. However the surviving papers show that within the Balkans Lt. Col. von Harling (by late 1943 the Ic at the headquarters of the Commander-in-Chief South-East, Army Group F which was the superior headquarters to Army Group E) was a regular and persistent correspondent on the subject of the 'Commando Order', challenging aspects of current practice, seeking clarification of policy and tirelessly advocating strict application of the spirit, if not the letter, of the Order.

On 19 May 1944 Army Group F contacted the OKW and stated that it believed that members of Allied Military Missions captured in the company of partisans should be handed over to the SD in accordance with the 'Commando Order'. This view apparently contradicted an earlier instruction from OKW in August 1943 that such persons be treated as prisoners of war since all captured partisans were allegedly being treated as prisoners of war. Army Group F sent a further signal on 1 June 1944 requesting clarification and stating that, until the matter was resolved, the members of such Missions would be handed over to the SD in accordance with the 'Commando Order'.

While this correspondence was underway, five British 'commandos' were captured on the Yugoslavian coastal island of Mljet on 22 May 1944 and handed over by the Army to the local Security Police (SIPO), although according to the SIPO it was the Army's job to deal with them. The Chief of Security Police and the SD in Belgrade took the view that the instructions in force in his area were that men of the AMM should be treated as prisoners of war. This view was supported by the authorities in Berlin because they considered that, where these men's functions were purely of an intelligence gathering nature and did not involve sabotage or terrorist activities, they did not fall within the terms of the 'Commando Order'. Further, the SD suggested that it was doubtful if the recent attack on Mljet by some 400 regular soldiers could be regarded as a 'commando' operation. A clear decision was sought in order to end the confusion and unnecessary work involved in considering such cases.

The SD sought to minimise its involvement in cases concerning 'commandos', challenging the Army's claim that the SD should deal with such men. It referred to the text of the 'Commando Order' and pointed out that the Army was negligent in taking the men prisoner rather than shooting them down in combat. Should some nevertheless survive, the SD contended that it was not their job to make good the Army's omission; SD responsibility according to its own interpretation of the 'Commando Order', lay only with individuals captured in the interior by police forces etc. On 1 July 1944 the Ic/AO Branch of Army Group F raised the matter of the five 'commandos' in a letter to the Reich Central Security Headquarters (RSHA) in Berlin, following up an earlier telegram of 17 June 1944. Army Group F sought to alter the RSHA's decision that the men be handed back to the Army and that they be treated as prisoners of war.

This correspondence led to general discussions in Berlin at the end of June between the relevant parts of the OKW and others such as the RSHA. The latter's view noted that the 'Commando Order' posed a threat of reciprocal action by the Allies against German Special Forces largely under RSHA control (those from the II Dept e.g. FAT 250) and they considered that the circumstances that gave rise to the 'Commando Order' no longer really existed. However the RSHA made no comment on the question of the treatment of AMM personnel. On 11 July 1944 the OKW summarised the positions of the different parties which were, with the exception of Army Group F, that only those engaged on 'commando' operations that coincided with both those described in the 'Commando Order' and those it was clearly meant to cover should be subject to its provisions; others should be treated as prisoners of war (Annexes 31–34).

A telephone enquiry from the OKW in mid-July 1944 to von Harling at Army Group F, as to whether British soldiers captured with the partisans had been subject to Sonderbehandlung, provided him with the opportunity to renew his complaint that the SD were not implementing the 'Commando Order' in such cases as the capture of five AMM men on the island of Brac in Yugoslavia (Annex 35). Further consideration of this subject within the OKW saw on 27 July 1944 a reiteration of the views put forward earlier in the month; but it was also recorded that Hitler was of the opinion that AMM personnel captured in the South-Eastern theatre should be treated as 'commandos'. This new development was reported to Army Group F by its Chief of Staff when he spoke to the staff on 20 July 1944. This made it clear that in the Balkan area oral orders had been given to units that they should 'despatch' any British or American troops found fighting with the partisans, or as 'commandos'. The Allies had to be made to realise that there was a price to pay for their support of the partisans (Annex 36). The official line on the AMM now changed: to reflect Hitler's wishes, a ruling was issued by Keitel the Head of the OKW soon after and was passed down from Army Group F to Army Group E on 17 August 1944 (Annex 37).

At about the same time von Harling seemed to win his point with reference to the Mljet captives. On the 18 August 1944 the OKW informed Army Group F that only the commander on the spot could effectively decide whether a particular operation was a 'commando' or a normal military operation (Annex 38). However, the question of the Mljet prisoners' fate was now somewhat academic as, during the period of this extended correspondence, the men had been passed into the standard prisoner of war system and were already in camps in Germany from which they were liberated at the end of the war (Annex 39).

In spite of the new policy laid down by the OKW, the SD were not, in their turn, to be moved. As correspondence from November 1944 reveals (Annex 40) they stressed that captured members of the AMM (however categorised), were not their responsibility. Attempts by von Harling to have this opposition overriden continued into early 1945 (Annex 41). Among the final surviving enclosures on the OKW file is a somewhat peremptory reply from the OKW in March 1945 instructing him to accept that the SD's decision, supported by the RSHA and Reichsführer SS in Berlin, was final and that the prisoners were to be accorded prisoner of war status (Annex 42).

This apparent reluctance on the part of some elements of the SD to act as the executioners of 'commandos', as in the case discussed above, is confirmed by the experience of Col. von dem Knesebeck (the Ic of 2 Panzer Army in Yugoslavia). In a recent statement for the Thames Television programme he said that, when he approached the local SD with reference to the disposal of other captured 'commandos', the SD officer concerned refused to accept them saying he was 'not a butcher' and that the SD was not bound by the 'Commando Order' which he claimed applied only to the Wehrmacht (3). It must not be assumed however that all members of the SD took this attitude to carrying out executions, or that the SD acted in this way out of concern for the prisoners. The activities of the SD in other areas, which led to its proscription as a 'criminal organisation' per se by the Allied post-war war crimes tribunals, are well recorded. One of the British post-war war crimes investigators who specialised in cases concerning the 'Commando Order' found evidence in other theatres of a desire by the SD to involve the German Armed Forces more closely in the disposal of 'commandos'. In the case of the execution of some Allied 'commandos' in France, the SD restricted their own role to ensuring compliance with the Order by escorting the firing squad which the Armed Forces had been made to provide.

Although Lt. Col. von Harling seems to have sought the implementation of the 'Commando Order', the Headquarters of Army Group F still seemingly sought to implement it in such a way as to avoid the loss of potentially valuable intelligence which would result from the immediate execution of 'commandos' as soon as they were encountered and from the refusal to take any prisoners which the Order required.

This is reflected in the War Diary of Army Group E which contains four references in March and April 1944 on the subject of the 'Commando Order'. Although the text of the first entry (in early March) has not survived, the reference merely being titled 'Handling of Enemy Sabotage Troops', the second entry (soon after in the same month) announced the annulment of the 'suspension provisions' to the 'Commando Order' that had been promulgated in the first reference, implying that this had attempted to modify the Order in some way (Annex 43). The third entry (of 16 March) set out the thinking behind Army Group F's view, namely that the need to obtain information from 'commandos'—about their organisation, bases and future plans in relation to the German-held islands—meant that the provisions of the 'Commando Order' for the disposal of captured 'commandos' should only be enforced after interrogation (Annex 44). This instruction was reinforced by a further order issued on 13 April by Army Group E which informed its subordinate formations that, in order to obtain the required information, captured 'commandos' were to be sent to the Army Group Headquarters after only a preliminary local interrogation. A decision on their further treatment with respect to the 'Commando Order' would be taken by the Army Group (Annex 45).

A document that has survived in the F papers outlined the discussions between the various Ics in the Army Group E area in the late spring or early summer of 1944. It probably records a tour of inspection either by von Harling from Army Group F himself or one of his officers who then advised him of the result. It sheds a revealing light on the views of the intelligence world on the interpretation and implementation of the 'Commando Order'. The formal, confidential and frank discussions demonstrate the Ics' concern over the loss of potentially valuable prisoners to interrogate by the strict implementation of the 'Commando Order'. The amendments to the 'Commando Order' mentioned above can be seen as part of a process to prevent such loss of intelligence: but clearly the amendment had caused some problems, as the document mentioned that a unit commander had objected to an attempted modification of the 'Commando Order' by the Army Group because he considered only the OKW and Hitler could amend a Führerbefehl. Therefore, the summary noted, that in order to avoid further incidents, when modifications or amendments to the 'Commando Order' were issued, they should be couched in such form as to disguise the fact that they did not come from the OKW (Annex 46).

This material also serves to demonstrate that the additional provisions of the covering letter to the 'Commando Order'—allowing temporary reprieve from execution to permit interrogation—were not widely known, perhaps the result of its limited distribution.

The extent to which von Harling's attitude influenced his subordinate intelligence officers, including those in Army Group E, remains an open question. The headquarters of Army Group E can hardly have been unaware of his views or at least his interest in 'commando' matters. A fragment of correspondence between von Harling and Lt. Col. Warnstorff, has survived and makes this point clear. In it, von Harling criticised Warnstorff for not keeping him properly informed about developments within his sphere of command concerning 'commandos' and their interrogation (Annex 47). Warnstorff's reply firmly rejected all suggestion of error on his part or that of Army Group E: but it does not reveal a degree of interest in the subject of the fate of 'commandos' equal to that taken by von Harling himself.

However, documentary evidence of opposition either to von Harling's policy or to the principles of the 'Commando Order' per se is lacking. There was no reluctance to report the activities of 'commandos' and their capture to higher authority. Moreover, the contemporary records demonstrate that the intelligence officers subordinate to von Harling opposed the implementation of the 'Commando Order' only because of the resultant loss of a valuable source of information. It should be remembered that there was widespread dislike within the German forces of partisan activity and this almost certainly extended at least in part to the 'irregular' operations of British 'commandos' and others who worked with the partisans. This feeling emerges in a recent comment to the Thames Television researchers by a German officer who served in the area: he spoke with apparent distaste of men who operated with blackened faces and knives in their hands to kill people from behind (4).

On the other hand, in recent oral testimony a number of German officers and NCOs from the Greek theatre have mentioned their dislike of the 'Commando Order' on moral and humanitarian grounds, particularly the thought of shooting uniformed troops captured in battle. There have been recent claims by various German officers that they sought to circumvent the requirements of the order by a variety of means apart from opposing it openly. The Ic of 2 Panzer Army (Col. von dem Knesebeck) has recently stated that he was able to protect 'commandos' by not reporting them as such. Another officer appears to have circumvented the order with the permission of his commanding General by 'accidentally' advising the Red Cross of the existence of two Allied Military Mission men in his hands (cf. p. 83). A similar claim is made by one of the NCOs in Army Group E's headquarters who recently stated that Lt. Col. Warnstorff personally approved such action for two 'commandos' under interrogation at Salonika (cf. p. 72). Warnstorff suggested in discussion with the Austrian Commission that perhaps one way to save individual 'commandos' from Sonderbehandlung was to draw out their journey as much as possible. He implied that his action with respect to one prisoner he met at Mitrovica was at least partially designed to achieve this effect (5).

It is difficult to know what credence to attach to these claims. If wholly accurate, they assume that 'accidental' notifications to the Red Cross and other 'slips' were accepted at face value by higher authority rather than as attempts to sabotage the 'Commando Order'. They have moreover to be compared with comments by other officers on the dangers of not carrying out a Führerbefehl. Lt. Col. Warnstorff commented to the Austrian Commission 'It was as good as committing suicide .... to oppose openly the Führerbefehl' (6). An officer based on Rhodes said in an interview for Thames Television 'What can he do? Nothing: there is the 'Commando Order', he cannot free the two men: he cannot say "I won't do this" ' (7).

However, on the surviving evidence Lt. Col. von Harling certainly appears to have been unique in the area under Army Group F in his apparent enthusiasm for the application of the 'Commando Order': the attitude of his subordinates is less clear.

In the event the fate of British 'commandos' captured in the area varied: some were apparently executed; others survived the war, even where in some cases they had been marked for Sonderbehandlung. The circumstances of the individual cases and the men's fate are examined in detail in Chapters 6–10.

Remarks on the German use of the term 'Sabotage'

The penultimate point to be addressed in considering the 'Commando Order' is the German use of the term 'sabotage' in their reports relating to the activities of 'commandos' and other British Special Forces including members of the Allied

Military Missions. This is of importance in relation to one of the cases concerning British servicemen examined later. From the evidence both of German reports of Allied 'commando' operations, and of the orders applying to German responses thereto, the Germans regarded as 'sabotage attacks' any operations not clearly linked to 'normal' on-going military actions. Where 'commando' attacks were of the hit and run variety or were in conjunction with the partisans, especially where demolitions were concerned, this was 'sabotage'.

This use of the term can be clearly traced from the original 'Commando Order' through other relevant documents, not only in the Balkan area, as a document from the Italian theatre confirms (Annex 48). Of interest in this context is the recent testimony of an NCO from the Army Group E Headquarters who describing Allied activities in the area, said that, whereas earlier they 'only went in for sabotage and sent sabotage troops who blew up bridges and so on', later more and more Allied officers were sent to help the partisan groups combine or at least operate more effectively (8). Clearly the Germans concerned saw, and in some cases still see, nothing strange about labelling such activities as 'sabotage'. The use of the term was therefore quite common and not of particular significance in relation to the categorization of prisoners captured while engaged in such operations. To the Germans in almost all cases such men were 'saboteurs' per se.

What did the Allies know of the Order?

From surviving Allied records it would appear that the significance of the Wehrmachtbericht of 7 October 1942, which like all similar broadcasts was routinely monitored in Britain, was not appreciated. At least there is no evidence that following the broadcast any immediate consideration was given to its implications for the treatment of Allied prisoners of war, notably those captured on 'commando' operations. Two further German communiques in late 1942 reported the destruction of 'sabotage' troops, in terms that can now be recognised as those mentioned in the covering letter to the 'Commando Order'.

> One Bomber and both Gliders were forced to land. The sabotage troops they were carrying were put to battle and wiped out to the last man.
>
> On the 8th December [1942] a small British sabotage squad was engaged at the mouth of the GIRONDE and was finished off in combat (9).

However, it was only when a report was received from agents in Norway that the men involved in the first incident, the abortive attack on the Vemork power station (Op Freshman), had been shot by the Germans after capture that Allied suspicions were aroused concerning German actions in such instances and the implications of the German communiques were somewhat better appreciated (Annex 49).

In the case of another group of 'commandos' captured in Norway, the standard German 'cover' line that they had been killed in battle or flight could not be used. The 'commandos' were being transported from the area, presumably for interrogation elsewhere, when one of them was seen and recognised by another British prisoner of war. Accordingly, although the men were executed in late October 1942, in January 1943 the German prisoner of war authorities responsible for informing the United Kingdom of any Britons made prisoners of war by the Germans were advised by the Reich Central Security Headquarters that they had 'escaped': a private enquiry from England received in Germany via the Red Cross elicited the same answer. Although prepared to broadcast that such forces had been eliminated in combat, the Germans seemed unwilling to admit to later executions away from the field of battle.

By early February 1943 British intelligence sources had provided fairly reliable information that 'the German military have received orders from high authority that all persons landing from aircraft to carry out sabotage are to be shot out of hand, irrespective of whether they are uniformed or not' (10). The problem was now formally considered by the Services. It was noted that, if the raids were halted, the Germans would have achieved their objective: therefore, that course should not be considered. It was however suggested that all men for such operations should be volunteers (as to a large extent they already were.)

In May 1943 the United Kingdom decided that the Germans should be approached through the Swiss authorities in a form designed to draw them into making a statement both on the facts of the Op Freshman case and on their general attitude to the treatment of such personnel, and to establish whether illegal shootings were being carried out on the authority of the German High Command. The Germans—in a prompt reply of 17 May 1943, apparently approved by Hitler himself—effectively admitted that such shootings were official policy and drew attention to the announcement in the Wehrmachtbericht of 7 October 1942. But they still did not mention belated execution of such men after interrogation (Annex 50).

The British authorities appear only at this juncture to have taken full note of the Wehrmachtbericht and after wide consultation advised the Germans of the illegal nature of their stated intentions in it. But the general UK view was that little could be done at that time to force the Germans to change their ways if such action was indeed a firm policy, something about which there still seems to have been some doubt.

Although the Allied wireless intercept and deciphering operations had recorded at least one German signal early in 1944 which referred to Sonderbehandlung in the context of Allied Special Forces personnel, this material was accorded the highest security classification at the time and dissemination of information obtained by this method was very strictly controlled in order to protect its source. The use of such information was limited to the most important operational plans. Therefore it is probable that information from this source was not passed to lower level operational headquarters or to the Service casualty organisations. In any case the signal gave no explanation or commentary on Sonderbehandlung and it should also be remembered that at that time the sinister reality behind the phrase Sonderbehandlung was unknown to the Allies.

The Germans' view expressed in the 'Commando Order' that British Special Forces personnel not engaged on 'commando' raids but aiding partisans were also not entitled to treatment as ordinary prisoners of war was known to the United Kingdom authorities by the summer of 1944 (Annex 51). This corresponded with the experience of the International Red Cross who in the Balkan theatre in mid 1944 recorded that some British troops captured in Greece were possibly being considered by the Germans as 'partisans' rather than as normal prisoners of war (Annex 52). Correspondence later the same year between Force 133 and MI9 confirms that general German attitudes on the status of 'commandos' or liaison personnel in the Balkans were then known:

> O'Neill's story saved him and he was treated as a POW. I arranged with the Red Cross to give him extra parcels of food etc. but no more, as to show that there was an organisation behind him would have disproved his story and been the cause of his death.
>
> GHQ recorded on 26 November 1944 the successful efforts made by the Swedish and Swiss Consuls and representatives in Athens and Salonika to ensure that the Germans did not execute the British prisoners of war concerned (11).
> [This refers to some of the cases discussed in Chapter 10].

However, it seems that execution was still not assumed to be the likely fate of any such personnel captured and this remained the general British view at least until late 1944 when rumours of the murder of SAS troops in Normandy, the capture of copies of German correspondence concerning the 'Commando Order', and evidence of executions under this instruction brought home to the Allies the full extent of the action the Germans were taking in such cases.

Eventually in March 1945 Gen. Eisenhower (the Supreme Allied Commander in Europe) issued a stern message via the BBC's transmitter at Daventry to the German forces, warning that they would be brought to account for any illegal actions against Allied personnel. He formally denounced the 'Führer Order' and the suggestion that uniformed soldiers could be regarded as 'terrorists'.

During the earlier part of this period there is no clear evidence that Special Forces and similar personnel were formally advised of the extra risk they ran as a result of German policy. However, some later comments from former Special Forces personnel suggest that the men were at some stage advised (either officially or unofficially) at least of the possible risk. This was certainly the case in the spring of 1945 in the Balkans when the commander of the Long Range Desert Group advised his men of the possible dangers as soon as the news from Normandy reached him (12).

CHAPTER 5: References

(1) War Office file in the Public Record Office (PRO) DEFE 2: 1126.

(2) Trials before US Military War Crimes Tribunal at Nuremberg: The OKW Trial.

(3) Thames Television: unbroadcast interview.

(4) Thames Television: unbroadcast interview.

(5) Thames Television: unbroadcast interviews and Austrian Commission interviews.

(6) Austrian Commission interview.

(7) Thames Television: unbroadcast interview.

(8) Thames Television.

(9) War Office file in PRO DEFE 2: 1126.

(10) Ibid.

(11) SOE archives.

(12) D. Lloyd Owen: Providence Their Guide. Harrap, London. 1980.

Chapter 6: The cases of British servicemen captured by the Germans in the Balkans which are examined in this Review. The Cephalonia Case

This chapter is the first of four (6-9) which examine those cases concerning the fifteen 'commandos' and Allied Military Mission personnel who are known to have been captured by the Germans in the area of the Balkans under the control of Army Group E during the period of Lt. Waldheim's service there as the O3 and which have been brought to the attention of the Ministry of Defence.

The Review also includes in Chapter 10 further cases relating to other British Special Forces personnel whom it has proved possible to identify as having been captured by the Germans in the relevant area and period. Although these have not been raised with the Ministry of Defence, they have been included for several reasons. It was important to ascertain whether or not the experiences and fate of the individuals concerned were of relevance in that they might involve Lt. Waldheim. Records dealing with the men and any British investigations into their fate might have revealed information of relevance to the main cases under review. It was important to establish, if possible, if a pattern existed in the Germans' treatment of such prisoners which might help clarify and disclose the possible responsibility for the events in the main cases.

Also included in Chapter 10 are cases involving non-Special Forces personnel which were also brought to the Ministry of Defence's attention. Some of those drawing attention to these cases have alleged that the personnel had suffered illegal treatment and that Lt. Waldheim was closely involved in their fate. This claim also applies to the case relating to British prisoners of war in Italy where specific allegations have been made against Lt. Waldheim concerning the death of some of these prisoners. To these cases have been added for completeness those of Special Forces personnel who were clearly in no way considered by the Germans to be 'commandos'.

For similar reasons to those given above, the Review has looked at other cases of non-Special Forces personnel captured in the area. With the exception of the case of Pte. Turton this has revealed no information relevant to the main cases nor any evidence of any illegal activity by the Headquarters of Army Group E, which would require these additional cases to be included in this Report.

It is not claimed that the case of every British serviceman who became a prisoner of war in the relevant area has been included. From the examination of contemporary German documents, it is clear that periodic returns of Allied servicemen captured give numbers but do not necessarily provide information about the units to which the servicemen belonged or any personal identification. Such reports include not only Special Forces personnel but also aircrew who had been forced to bale-out over the area, as well as any 'evaders' or escapers from the servicemen left behind after the 1941 campaign in Greece. A contemporary report by the British service escape and evasion organisation for the area recorded its awareness that in March 1944 there were between 400 and 500 British,

Commonwealth and American escapees/evaders at liberty in Greece. This figure does not include the several thousands of others who had already passed into German captivity.

The cases concerning British Special Forces personnel which have been brought to the Ministry of Defence's attention have been examined in separate Chapters. These are:

Chapter 6. The Cephalonia party; Capt. Warren.

Chapter 7. The Alimnia party; Capt. Blyth, Sub/Lt. Tuckey, L/Sgt. Miller, Gnr. Jones, Pte. Evans, Pte. Rice, Telegraphist Carpenter.

Chapter 8. The Yannina party; Capt. Hamilton, Capt. Bluett, Gnr. Bennett, Pte. Davies.

Chapter 9; The Calino party; Sgt. Dryden, Pte. Doughty, Pte. Fishwick.

The additional cases including those of British Special Forces personnel identified during the Review's research and those cases of non-Special Forces personnel that were brought to the Ministry of Defence's attention are examined in Chapter 10.

THE CEPHALONIA CASE

This section concerns the party of Allied and other personnel called here the 'Cephalonia party' which consisted of one British officer, one USAAF officer and three Polish and fifteen Russian deserters from German service.

The British officer was Capt. D. A. La. T. Warren, Royal Northumberland Fusiliers, who did not survive the war. The allegations in this case concerning the then Lt. Waldheim are that he was personally involved in the interrogation and general treatment of Capt. Warren, and that he prepared a report on Capt. Warren's interrogation in which he falsely described Capt. Warren as a saboteur thus bringing him within the terms of the 'Commando Order' so that he was subject to Sonderbehandlung and was executed.

Capt. Warren joined SOE (Force 133) at the beginning of June 1943 and after the usual training was dropped into Greece on 'Operation Coachman XXIV' on or about 10 August 1943. In the early part of 1944 Capt. Warren was in charge of 'Operation Conjugal' which involved the evacuation by caique to Italy of a party of fifteen Russian and three Polish deserters from German service plus one USAAF officer. The caique with its passengers and a Greek crew of three sailed on 20 or 21 March 1944 from Galaxidhion in Greece but before reaching the Italian coast the fuel for the motor ran out. There is a suggestion that either the money given for fuel had not all been used for that purpose or that some of the fuel had been sold. However the then Head of Force 133 in Greece (Col. Woodhouse) now considers that this explanation is unsatisfactory as he believes that there was no other case of such deliberate mis-use of funds during his service there (1).

In bad weather the caique was blown back towards Greece and at about 1200 hours on 25 March 1944 it either ran aground or was intercepted by a German naval vessel off the coast of Cephalonia near Cape Munda, the south-eastern point of the island. Before the Germans could board the caique, one of the Russians jumped overboard and swam ashore. In spite of enemy gunfire, he evaded capture and subsequently made contact with Maj. Ramseyer another member of the Allied Military Mission in the area. The remainder of the party were taken prisoner by the Germans. The following account of the captured members of the party is taken primarily from German documentary sources.

On 25/26 March 1944 a message from the Operational Staff (Ia) Corps Joannina* (later XXII (Geb) Korps) to Army Group E Operational Staff (Ia), also copied to the E Intelligence Staff (Ic), stated:

> 25 March midday on Cephalonia, off Cape Munda (South-East point of the island) twenty British soldiers probably sabotage party—captured. Further details not yet reported (Annex 53).

Already, and by a lower level headquarters, this party was regarded as 'saboteurs'. At 1330 on 26 March 1944 the Operations Staff (Ia) of HQ Army Group E sent its Daily Situation Report to its superior HQ Army Group F, High Command South East at Belgrade. This included a summary of the news from Cephalonia:

> Corps Joannina: On South-east point of Cephalonia, twenty men, probably British sabotage party, captured (Annex 54).

Early on 27 March 1944, Corps Joannina sent its Morning Report to Army Group E. From now on within Army Group E the reports of this matter went through the Ic—(intelligence)—net. The Joannina Ic report expanded somewhat on the Cephalonia prisoners:

> The sabotage party captured on 25 March 1944 (see Daily Report of 26 March) consisted of British, Americans, Russians and Poles. Weapons: two machine guns, various sub-machine guns and pistols. Short interrogation intended on 27 March 1944 in Patras. Onward passage of prisoners to Army Group with captured papers probably on 27 March 1944 (Annex 55).

This information was clearly passed on by Army Group E to Army Group F, as the latter's Daily Report to the OKW at 2130 hours on the night of 27 March 1944 supplemented a report it had submitted on this subject on 26 March 1944 and passed on this fresh information in the following form:

> Sabotage party on Cephalonia, [see daily sitrep for 26.3] consisted of British, Americans, Poles and Russians; weapons two machine guns, sub-machine guns and pistols. Movement to location for interrogation will be by plane weather permitting, then Sonderbehandlung in accordance with the Führerbefehl (Annex 56).

This signal from F is the first known mention of the 'Commando Order' and Sonderbehandlung in this case.

The Morning Report from Corps Joannina to Army group E for 28 March 1944, sent at 2310 hours 27 March 1944, gave details of the information gleaned from the initial interrogation of the prisoners.

* This is the German spelling of Yannina.

> Sabotage party Cephalonia from a motorised sailing boat under the Greek flag having allegedly left the Gulf of Corinth on 21 March with the aim of reaching Italy. One member of the party escaped [presumably the Russian who dived overboard]. The English Captain who landed by parachute on the night 23 March 1944 refuses to answer questions (Annex 57).

Capt. Warren was apparently deploying a cover story or disinformation here in describing his own movements.

The Army Group E evening report of 28 March 1944 to Army Group F provides a more detailed statement on the prisoners.

> The sub-unit (twenty) men forced to land on Cephalonia, comprises one British Army Captain, one American 2/Lt, one American civilian, Russians and Poles. They were en route from Galaxidhion (17.5 kms South of Amphyssa) to Italy. The Russians and Poles were apparently recruited by the Allies for service with the Allied exile [i.e. 'Free' Polish] forces and are therefore not commando troops. As the Poles and Russians had been German Army and service personnel they have been handed over to the GFP (Annex 58).

These details would suggest that Army Group E had by then received the prisoners and had given them at least a preliminary interrogation, correctly identifying the origin of the Russians and Poles. It is not clear whether the statement that the Russians and Poles were not 'commando troops' was designed to save them from the Sonderbehandlung foreshadowed in Army Group F's earlier signal, or was simply a correction of the earlier mistaken identification. However, as deserters they were handed over to the GFP. At this time Lt. Waldheim was still on leave in Austria having left the Headquarters on 25 February 1944.

No further surviving German documentary material has been found on this case until 8 April 1944 when the situation report from Corps Joannina to Army Group E mentions the Cephalonia party in its March listing of enemy casualties (Annex 59).

German contemporary documents next discuss the party on 8 May 1944 when Maj. Hammer, the AO of the Ic/AO Branch of Headquarters Army Group E and the deputy of the Ic (Lt. Col. Warnstorff), signed a report for onward transmission to Army Group F detailing the Ic/AO's assessment of the information gleaned from the interrogation of the Cephalonia prisoners, including Capt. Warren. This report is marked at its end with a 'W' and, therefore, it is believed that it was drafted by Lt. Waldheim who had returned from leave on about the 16 April 1944 (Annex 60).

While this document was in American hands after the war it was subject to 'masking' of some details, hence the obliterations in the text. (The reasons for this masking are discussed in the chapter concerning the relevant surviving records (cf. p. 107). However a partial reconstruction of the document has been possible (Annex 61).

The report sets out the background of the members of the party including brief notes on Capt. Warren's basic military career and role within the Allied Military Mission in Greece. In discussing the latter, it notes that Warren was not a member of a specialist Engineer unit but that he had received a special 'technical' training. The implication here is that the use of explosives and demolitions formed part of this training. This is correct: Force 133 personnel did receive basic training in these skills before starting operations. The report would seem to be based at least in part on Warren's own comments because some of the information (e.g. his service in North Africa) must have come from him. Further, although it is apparent that he was giving his interrogators only what information he considered of no great value to them and was refusing to elaborate on his real activities or matters of substance, it seems likely that Warren himself made some comment similar to that given in the report about the capabilities of the Greeks with regard to demolition matters; there is nothing to suggest that the Headquarters of Army Group E made deliberately inaccurate assessments of evidence. The comment was:

> Warren believed that the Greeks were too unreliable to be entrusted with sabotage operations on their own.

These comments could have been taken to imply that Warren himself did undertake sabotage, and this could explain why he was excluded when the remaining members of the party were taken out of the saboteurs category. As has already been seen in the chapter on the 'Commando Order', the Germans viewed any such operations outside the main battlefront as 'sabotage', regardless of whether or not some of the participants were regular military troops in uniform.

From other information obtained during the interrogation, presumably from the Russians and Poles, the Ic/AO Branch judged that a well organised network of agents existed in and around Athens, all receiving support from the British. This, and the final suggestion that the Russians in the group were later to be sent back to Greece for various tasks, were not in fact in accord with British resources and intentions: although the SOE had planned to segregate and train as agents some Russians captured while in German service, the plan had not been implemented. Whilst no major Allied offensive was planned against the Balkans, the Germans seriously thought otherwise. Their fears of an Allied attack in the area were known to the Allies who put considerable efforts into playing on these fears through deception schemes. There is no reason to believe that, on the main points, the interrogation report deliberately exaggerated the position as the Germans saw it.

Contemporary British accounts, based on messages passed through the partisans, reported that Capt. Warren and all the party except three Russians, one Pole, one Italian and two Greek members of the ship's crew, had been flown by seaplane to Athens, supposedly on 24 April 1944. The other personnel were taken to the nearest local German headquarters. The capture of the party was also reported by another British officer in the area on a special operation (Annex 62).

The Allied wireless intercept and deciphering operations had decoded the Army Group F report of 27 March 1944 which both mentioned the group and raised the prospect of Sonderbehandlung (Annex 63). But such material was accorded the highest security classification at the time and dissemination of information obtained by this method was very strictly controlled in order to protect its source. Therefore it is probable that the details concerning the party obtained from this source were not passed to the lower level operational headquarters, let alone to the Service casualty organisation.

The British obtained further information in late 1944 from one of the two Russians in the party who survived and later made contact with the Allies in Salonika. He stated that, on the party's arrival in Salonika on a date unknown, they were taken to what they believed to be a Gestapo prison or PW camp. This was almost certainly in fact the GFP Prison in the town. The party was apparently then split up and the Russian said that he had been beaten 'on and off' for two days, presumably during interrogations. He knew that Capt. Warren had attempted to dig a tunnel out of his cell but that this had been detected before it was complete.

He and the other Russian who escaped from the party added that Capt. Warren was removed from his cell by the Germans at about 2200 hours on what was believed to be 15 May 1944, and that he left all his belongings in his cell: Capt. Warren was never seen again in the camp. Although neither was a witness to the event, the Russians believed that he had been executed on the grounds that:

(i) prisoners for execution were normally removed at that time of night.

(ii) he took nothing with him: presumably he would have taken some belongings if he was only being transferred to another camp (Annex 64).

A further report was received in 1945 from an Allied Military Mission officer that, whilst a prisoner in German hands, a Greek partisan officer told him that a British officer had been taken to 'No 510 Gestapo' prison in Salonika and between 15 and 20 May 1944 had been condemned to death and shot by the Germans. The description provided by the Greek tallied in every detail with that of Capt. Warren whom the AMM officer knew well (Annex 65). An American officer was apparently also removed at the same time, again it was believed for execution. However, it has not proved possible to find any surviving records of any investigations into his fate which might have shed light on the fate of Warren.

Although the presumed execution of Capt. Warren was known to the Allied authorities in 1944, there is no evidence that any formal war crimes investigation was ever started in this case, although consideration was given to such action. According to Col. Woodhouse, the Head of Force 133 in Greece who remained in Greece with the British mission after the liberation, the situation there was very confused and difficult (2). This may well have influenced any decision on this matter, the more so as SOE itself was being run down very quickly and the small remaining staff were primarily concerned with the resettlement and administration of SOE's local personnel and helpers.

The formal acceptance of Capt. Warren's death whilst in enemy hands took place at the end of July 1945 and the available information was passed to his next-of-kin.

CHAPTER 6: References

(1) Discussion Col. Woodhouse/MOD.

(2) Ibid.

Chapter 7: The Alimnia Case

This section concerns the party of Allied Servicemen known as the 'Alimnia Party' which consisted of:

a. **Special Boat Section**

Capt. H. W. Blyth, Scots Guards.
L/Sgt. G. W. J. Miller, RAC (County of London Yeomanry).
Gnr. G. W. R. Jones, Royal Artillery.
Pte. L. G. Rice, Bedfordshire & Hertfordshire Regt.
Pte. A. G. Evans, Sherwood Foresters Regt.

b. **Naval Party (i.e. crew of Levant Schooner 24-LS24)**

Sub/Lt. A. L. Tuckey, RNVR.
Telegraphist R. E. Carpenter, RN.

c. **Greek Naval Personnel**

M. Lisgaris.
D. Triandaphillou.
N. Velisariu.

Of this party only one man (Capt. Blyth) is known to have survived the war. The allegation against Lt. Waldheim is that, in relation to this party of men, he was personally involved in and perhaps gave the order or relayed the orders to transfer them to the SD, resulting in their execution.

The following account is based on contemporary British and German records as well as those from the British post-war investigations. The majority of the German records come from a file specifically created by the Ic/AO Branch of Army Group F to cover the 'Alimnia' case. The relevant files from Army Group E and subordinate formations, with a few small exceptions, have not survived wartime destruction.

As part of the Allied Aegean raiding operations in the early months of 1944, 'Operation Fireater' involved the despatch of patrols from the SBS and other raiding forces to various islands in the Aegean. The patrols were usually transported on caiques of the Levant Schooner Flotilla, although on occasion Motor Torpedo Boats or Motor Launches were used.

The task of P patrol of S Detachment of the SBS (consisting of Capt. Blyth, L/Sgt. Miller, Gnr. Jones, Pte. Evans and Pte. Rice) was to land on the islands of Calchi and Alimnia. There they were to reconnoitre for suitable sites for caiques to use as a staging point in a future operation against German radar sites that had been requested by GHQ MEF in Cairo. They were not inexperienced soldiers: for example, Capt. Blyth had been with the SAS for some time, having been its Adjutant under Lt. Col. David Stirling, the Regiment's renowned creator.

The SBS patrol's transport to the area was the Levant Schooner number 24 (LS24) captained by Sub/Lt. Tuckey with Telegraphist Carpenter as his wireless operator and four Greek crew. Sub/Lt. Tuckey had joined the Levant Schooner Flotilla in January 1944 and, according to a contemporary British naval report, had already taken LS24 out on a reconnaissance mission between 30 March and 3 April 1944. Tuckey re-joined the vessel for this mission: the Greek captain had fallen sick and had gone ashore for treatment, as had another injured member of the crew. Carpenter joined the vessel on the day of their departure.

LS24 left the Raiding Forces base near Castelrosso about 1630 hours on the evening of 5 April 1944. Carpenter's diary records LS24's arrival at another Allied post at Loryma, opposite Rhodes about 0415 hours on 6 April 1944 and its departure at about 2000 hours on the same day. There is some confusion in the British records as to whether the party actually landed on Calchi. However, from the statements made by the Greek crew when interrogated by the Germans, it would seem that the boat hove-to just outside the harbour but, as a result of a radio message, no landing was made and the boat set sail for Alimnia which was reached at about 0200 hours on 7 April 1944. The Germans noted that these facts were supported by an entry in the ship's radio log. Having reached Alimnia, the SBS party went ashore to reconnoitre while the vessel's crew rested.

The German records indicate that sometime on 6 April 1944 a local agent in German service (called by the Germans a 'V-Mann') warned the German area command on Rhodes that British 'commandos' intended to land on the island of Calchi. As a result, that night German forces were warned to prepare for operations on the islands of Calchi and Alimnia. The forces earmarked for this mission were elements of the 1st Küstenjäger Brandenberger* (the 'Coastal-Patrol' Company of the Brandenburg Regiment): this unit had been raised from the special operations unit, the Brandenbergers, in the Spring of 1944 in order to combat the Allied 'commandos' operating in the Aegean. Lacking sufficient suitable vessels of their own, the Brandenbergers had in some instances, this being one, to use as well the boats of the local Army Engineer Landing Company. Escorts were usually provided by naval vessels.

On 7 April some of the German boats left the harbour of Castello on the west coast of Rhodes, carrying a landing party from the Brandenbergers. They were to clear the island of Calchi under the protection of two Submarine-hunters from the Navy. After landing the Brandenbergers on Calchi, the boats returned to Castello. About 0630 on the same day four 'assault boats' put to sea for Alimnia with a second landing party of Brandenbergers. This group was escorted by the motorship Malona from the Rhodes flotilla. The task of this group was to occupy the island of Alimnia, search it for British 'commandos' and set up strongpoints.

As the German party entered the harbour of Alimnia at about 0730, a British motor cutter at anchor at a small pier in a little cove was detected (despite being well camouflaged) to the starboard of the incoming German boats. The order of the boats was 'Caesar', 'Fritz', 'Dora' and 'Otto', with the 'Malona' bringing up the rear. As the leading German boat was about 300m from the camouflaged vessel, the Germans saw five armed soldiers in British uniforms (i.e. Tuckey, Carpenter and the three Greek sailors) leave the boat and take up defensive positions on the pier. The Germans simultaneously opened fire with the 20mm cannon and the machine guns on board 'Caesar'. During the short firefight which

* In a contemporary British SBS report, this German unit was likened to the SBS itself.

followed one German and two of their opponents (both Greeks) were wounded before the British party surrendered. Two of the German boats ('Caesar' and 'Fritz') laid themselves along the starboard side of the pier. Two British naval personnel one a naval Lieutenant, the other a radio-operator and three Greek sailors (also in British uniforms) were captured. The fourth member of the Greek crew had gone ashore to sleep and was not captured. There were two radios on the boat and, although the British radio operator had thrown his signal codes and instructions into the water before capture, these were recovered by the Germans.

During the brief exchange of fire, the other two assault boats carried on towards the shore some 400m east of the pier in order to land their troops to carry out the task of sweeping the island to the high ground at 'Point 123'. The German platoon commander briefly saw at least one British soldier eastwards of Point 123 as his group landed. He was however ordered to take his remaining troops and the machine guns to join the force commander by the pier. The British boat (called by the Germans a 'cutter') was then searched. After this a signal was sent to the Headquarters at Rhodes informing them of the capture of the boat and 'British commando troops'. At about 0830 the motorboat 'Malona'—the crew having being reinforced by two men with a machine gun—was despatched with the five prisoners to Rhodes, with the additional task of checking on any fishing boats seen en route. The Brandenbergers were now combing the island, without any result. However, from the high ground of Point 123 the platoon commander saw that the 'Malona', having sailed on a north-east course for about thirty minutes, had sighted a fishing boat that was on course for Turkey.

According to the post-war testimony in 1945 of the Greek fisherman on this boat, they had arrived at Alimnia from Calchi with about 5–600 kilos of fish. They were approached by a British 'Corporal' who asked them to help him and his comrades, to which they agreed. The Corporal boarded the boat and one of the Greeks disembarked. On reaching the spot on the island's coast where the remainder of the British party were—described incorrectly by the Greeks as a 'naval' officer and three other soldiers, although the party were in fact all SBS—the Greeks suggested that they hide the five men until dark. However the British seemed to be in a great hurry to get away and, perhaps misunderstanding what was said to them, insisted on leaving immediately and started emptying the boat of its contents, throwing some things into the sea. The boat had set sail in a north-easterly direction towards the nearest point of Turkey when it was overtaken by the German boat. The German boat fired a shot across the bows of the sailing boat which 'hove to'.

According to the Greek fishermen the Germans were at first prepared to let them pass but then made a second check and found the British servicemen. On the German commander removing several tarpaulins, he found five British servicemen lying there. These (a Captain and four soldiers) were disarmed and transferred to the German vessel which, taking the other boat in tow, sailed for Rhodes, arriving at about 1400 hours. There the wounded and prisoners were handed over to Maj. Kronsbein the Ia (Operations officer) of the Rhodes Division. The two wounded Greeks from the British boat were taken to hospital.

The signals that were sent at that time from Rhodes to Army Group E have not survived. The Daily Situation Report from Army Group E at 1330 on 7 April said only that, in the area under command of the Rhodes Division, a platoon of the Brandenbergers had landed on Alimnia and a further German raiding party had landed on Calchi (Annex 66). (At this time Lt. Waldheim was on leave in Austria).

On 8 April the Daily Situation Report sent out by the Rhodes Headquarters Operations Staff (Ia) gave Army Group E more details of the incident referred to in the earlier report, also issued on the Ia net. Unfortunately, as already mentioned, the earlier report has not survived.

The 8 April report stated that, according to the prisoners' statements, the task of the British was only to establish whether Alimnia or Calchi were garrisoned by the Germans and that the party had arrived at Alimnia only a few hours before the arrival of the Brandenbergers. The starting point for the 'English commandos' was Castelrosso and a detailed evaluation of their interrogation was to follow by courier (Annex 67). The fact that the lower level commanders (i.e. those on Rhodes) called the British party 'commandos' from the outset suggests that, given the nature of the party's mission and method of operation, their designation as such was a routine reaction as far as the Germans were concerned. Although the consequences of such designation in terms of the 'Commando Order' were known at levels of command such as these, their action displays no evident concern to disguise the true nature of the prisoners, contrary to subsequent claims.

The basic details of the capture of the 'commandos' were passed on by Army Group E to HQ, Army Group F in the Daily Report at 1330 hours on 8 April 1944 (Annex 68).

This report mentioned a total of twelve men captured, which figure of course included the Greek fishermen on the boat carrying the SBS party captured at sea.

Meanwhile, on arrival at the port of Castello on Rhodes during the afternoon of 7 April 1944, the two officers (Capt. Blyth and Sub/Lt. Tuckey) were at once separated from the other ranks of the British party and driven by car to the German Divisional Headquarters. The other ranks were taken to the town gaol of Rhodi, the main town of Rhodes. The officers were given a meal and questioned separately by Maj. Kronsbein, with Sgt. Viebrock acting as interpreter. Tuckey was questioned first. The two officers spent that night in different buildings. Blyth briefly saw Tuckey again about noon the next day, but not to speak to; he also heard his voice in another room.

In the afternoon of 8 April 1944 Blyth was flown to Athens and thence to the special interrogation centre co-located with Stalag VIIA at Moosburg in Germany for further interrogation. This was presumably because, as the leader of the SBS party, he was considered to be the prisoner with the greatest knowledge of 'commando' matters and Allied intentions in the theatre. From later correspondence it is evident that the decision to move him to Moosburg was taken by Army Group E without consulting Army Group F in Belgrade (cf. p. 53).

Meanwhile on Rhodes Sgt. Viebrock accompanied Lt. Lochner (the O3 to the Ic, Lt. Brenner, who was apparently not on the island at the time) to the town gaol. There on 8 April 1944 they interrogated the other ranks. (In contrast to Army Group level, (cf. p. 20) within the smaller Divisional Headquarters prisoner interrogation was it seems a task for the O3). Meanwhile Lochner had been given a 'Movement Order' to send the prisoners to the airfield and hand them over to Maj. Kronsbein. Accordingly on the following morning Viebrock was ordered to collect the other ranks from the gaol and convey them to the airfield at Marrizza and there hand them over to Maj. Kronsbein. Due to delays on the journey this was not achieved. The next day he tried again but on this occasion 'lost' the prisoners en route to the airfield and was threatened by Maj. Kronsbein with Court-Martial if the prisoners escaped. Eventually the prisoners did arrive at the airfield but too late for the flight, so they were returned yet again to the gaol. The next day, 11 April 1944, Viebrock did succeed in getting the prisoners to the airfield in time. He handed them over to Maj. Kronsbein who had been ordered to fly with them to Salonika to Army Group E's Headquarters and to hand them over to the Ic of the Army Group (Lt. Col. Warnstorff): this he duly did. According to a post-war statement by Sgt. Viebrock, Army Group E had sent Gen. Löhr's own aircraft as it would make the journey in one flight whereas the usual transport aircraft had to make stops en route (1).

This sequence of events fits what seems to have been the normal pattern within the area under Army Group F—this was that all members of 'commandos' or other special forces had to be handed over to the Army Group HQ which, when thought appropriate, then passed them on to the special interrogators of the OKH (some of whom were based at Moosburg). As mentioned earlier (cf. p. 32), in order to gain intelligence, Army Group F had ordered E and its subordinate formations to take prisoner 'commandos' but after interrogation to dispose of them in accordance with the 'Commando Order'. This routine for handling such prisoners was confirmed by Maj. Kronsbein and Gen. Kleeman, (the Commanding General on Rhodes) during post-war interrogations on this subject (2).

On the same day (11 April 1944) Blyth's movement to Moosburg was reported to Army Group F by Army Group E in a letter with which was enclosed a copy of the report of Blyth's interrogation on Rhodes (Annex 69). However, owing to the time taken for letters to get from Salonika to Belgrade, these documents were not received at F until 15 April 1944.

About this time the Greek fishermen captured with Blyth's party were released as the British had convinced the Germans that they had forced the Greeks to help them at gun point.

On 12 April 1944, the German official military news radio broadcast from Berlin, the Wehrmachtbericht covering the events of 11 April 1944, announced that a 'commando' force attempting to land on Rhodes had been wiped out:

> 11 April 1944: Das Oberkommando der Wehrmacht gibt bekannt . . . Ein an der Westküste von Rhodos gelandeter britischer Kommandotrupp wurde im Kampf bis auf den letzten Mann niedergemacht.

> The German High Command reports . . . A British commando unit which landed on the west coast of Rhodes was engaged and eliminated down to the last man.

This was of course the standard form of words set down in the covering letter to the 'Commando Order' for use in reporting 'commando raids'.

The Operations staff in Army Group E signalled to Army Group F on the 13 April asking for permission to take advantage of the information about the location of British 'commando' bases in Turkish territorial waters, and the details of the recognition signals etc, by using the Coastal Patrol Company of the Brandenbergers to destroy some of the 'commando' bases on the otherwise unoccupied Turkish islands: preparations, they said, were already in hand (Annex 70). As the proposed attacks were an operational matter, this signal went to the Operations staff of Army Group F who passed the suggestion on to the OKW (Annex 71). The Ic/AO Branch in F did not receive a copy until the next day (14 April). E's signal is recorded in the War Diary which also records the despatch by the Ic/AO Branch in E of a letter to F (almost certainly as the result of a comment by Rhodes) stating that, with the capture of LS24, valuable material in the form of British recognition signals and radio codes had fallen into their hands. These, they felt, would have enabled the Germans to decipher British naval radio traffic in the eastern Mediterranean area until 15 April when the codes changed. Further, the recognition signals could have been available for future operations of the Brandenbergers. But the Wehrmachtbericht on 11 April, in revealing that the 'commandos' had fallen into German hands, had nullified possible use of the signal traffic for future operations by the Coastal Patrol Company against British 'commando' bases (Annex 72). The Ic section at F noted against E's last point that in future in reporting such items their unsuitability for inclusion in the Wehrmachtbericht should be indicated. In fact, once the loss of the now overdue LS24 was assumed, the British Raiding Forces switched automatically to other codes which were not compromised. Indeed a British naval officer who served at the time with the Raiding Forces has recently commented that the Germans had attempted to use the captured radio codes but that their attempts had been detected (3). Certainly the German broadcast, which was monitored by the British, was felt to be too much of a coincidence. Accordingly, Maj. Sutherland (the officer commanding S Detachment SBS) sent a two-man party to Calchi during the night 13/14 April to investigate, but their attempts to land were foiled by bad weather on a succession of nights and they returned to base having failed to achieve their mission. However, as the capture of LS24 was a possibility and there was therefore a danger that the rest of the SBS Detachment had been compromised, on 14 April 1944 the planned operation against the radar stations was postponed indefinitely. The next day, in order to avoid any possible German counter-strike, the base was moved to another location although it remained in Turkish territorial waters. In fact a German naval signal of 10 April 1944 (repeating a German report of 1800 hours of 9 April which reported the capture of LS24) had been intercepted and decoded by the British but, as with other information gained from this source, there is no evidence that this information was passed to the low level commanders (Annex 73).

On 14 April 1944 one of the Ic staff of HQ Army Group F (Lt. Heinicke*) spoke to Sonderführer Paschiera, one of the interpreters in the F branch, and asked for answers to a number of questions concerning the Alimnia prisoners by 10 o'clock the next morning. The Sonderführer in turn passed the questions to HQ Army Group E by telephone:

1. Where are the men?
2. Already interrogated?
3. Interrogation completed?
4. When [are they to be given] Special Treatment?

The reply from Lt. Krohne and Lt. Poliza was:

1. They are with E [i.e. with us.]
2. Interrogation not yet completed (very obstinate)
3. The men are to be handed over to the SD early tomorrow, and are to be further interrogated there. The date for Sonderbehandlung will be decided by the SD.

The record of this conversation, preserved in Army Group F's files, was signed by Sonderführer Paschiera, at 1900 hours on the 14 April (Annex 74). This is the first mention of Sonderbehandlung in files relating to the Aliminia 'commandos' and it arose as a result of this telephone conversation. Thus, it seems that a decision had already been taken in principle that the party should be subject to Sonderbehandlung at a time when Lt. Waldheim was still on leave in Austria.

At 1335 hours the same day the Ic/AO Branch at E sent a signal to F outlining the details so far obtained from the interrogations. As the only surviving copy is from the F file, it bears no personal authorisation or signature from the sender in E, only the 'block' authorisation of the Ic/AO Branch. This information was passed by F to OKW and OKH on the same day (Annex 75).

The next day the initial signal was transcribed by F to make it more clear (Annex 76) and translations of several of the abbreviations were provided by the staff of the F Ic/AO Branch. (It was about this time that Lt. Waldheim returned to Army Group E from his leave in Austria).

In the GCHQ archive there is a reference to a decrypt of an intercepted German military message from Army Group E to Rhodes on the 15 April 1944 which said that, in spite of the earlier orders, the two British and three Greek sailors belonging to the British 'commando' force captured on Alimnia were to be flown to Salonika at once. This suggests that the two British naval personnel and the Greek seamen were not initially sent to Salonika with the remaining SBS men but followed later. This initial distinction between the prisoners by Army Group E is quite logical as the Germans' main interest was in the organisation and role of the

* The F Ic/AO Branch organisation chart (Annex 223) shows Lt. Heinicke as being responsible for coverage of the enemy situation in the north Balkans, not for the Allied Forces area.

SBS as a 'commando' force, as well as their future plans. The change of plan in the movement of the non-SBS elements recorded here was probably also a result of F's intervention shown in the telephone enquiry already mentioned.

On 16 April 1944 Lt. Col. Warnstorff (the Ic of Army Group E) signed a letter to his superior Lt. Col. von Harling (the Ic in F) which set out formally the circumstances of the capture of the 'commandos' and provided an analysis of the information contained in the captured papers. Also included were the captured papers on recognition signals etc plus translations; examples of the cap insignia worn by the SBS men; a report on the British weapons; the instructions for the Greek ship's captain with translation; the diary of the British radio operator with translation; and various other captured papers (Annex 77). However, this package, the despatch of which was also recorded in the Morning Report (Annex 78), was not received by F until 20 April. Copies of this information were also distributed by Warnstorff both to E's own Operations Branch—Ia—and to the naval and air liaison officers in E for further distribution to their respective services. Some of the particular papers which contain details of the recognition signals were not kept by F in its file. The E file copy was passed to its operations branch (Ia) (Annex 79).

At 1120 hours on the same day (16 April) while this package was en route to Army Group F, the Operations Staff in Headquarters Army Group F received from the OKW a reply to their signal of 14 April putting forward the suggestions of E for action against the 'commando' bases in Turkish waters. The answer stated that Hitler had not approved the proposed attack on 'commando' bases in Turkish waters but that for the time being the witnesses of British violations of Turkish neutrality should be kept available (Annex 80). Lt. Strnad (the F 07 Ordonnanz Offizier) noted that the suggested approach to Turkey should await the outcome of further investigations.

The letter from E advising of Capt. Blyth's transfer direct from Rhodes to Moosburg had now arrived. The next day (16 April) F signalled Stalag VIIA at Moosburg (here called Lückenwalde, another title for the same camp) requesting that Capt. Blyth, who had been sent to Moosburg from Rhodes, should be passed to the SD in accordance with the 'Führerbefehl of 18.10.42' (the 'Commando Order'). Von Harling directed that the SD be asked to hold him at the disposal of the OKH; his interrogation was to take place as instructed by the OKH (Annex 81). Simultaneously von Harling notified the OKW of this fact, adding that he considered that, though Blyth was as yet uncommunicative, he should be well informed about the organisation, strength, distribution and operational possibilities of the Raiding Forces. In fact, Blyth's further interrogation had already been carried out by the professional Army interrogators. A copy of the resultant report was dated 16 April 1944, the same day as von Harling's intervention: this report was sent from Moosburg to OKW rather than direct to F.

Significantly, on the copy of the report of the initial interrogation of Capt. Blyth on Rhodes, which had been forwarded by E, arriving at F 15 April 1944 and which von Harling now sent on to the OKH and OKW, von Harling added a short note recording Blyth's transfer to Moosburg and the fact that transfer to the SD had been ordered (Annex 82).

Blyth however was not passed to the SD but into the routine prisoner of war administrative chain and was sent to an ordinary prisoner of war camp where he remained until his liberation at the end of the war.

On 18 April 1944 Ic F signalled E repeating the information regarding the Führer's rejection of the proposed raids on the 'commando' bases in Turkey. The signal added that it was necessary, as soon as possible after successful interrogation, to prepare evidence of the presence of Allied bases in Turkish waters which could be passed to the Turkish government and that witnesses of this should be kept. Further it stated that this matter was now to be exclusively an Ic matter (intelligence) and that Ia (operations) were to be advised of this (Annex 83). It has been suggested that the mention of it as an 'Ic' matter excluded the 'AO'. In fact this signal only indicates that, as the projected attack on the bases had been forbidden, this matter was no longer of operational interest and the Ia branch was no longer to be involved; the Ic/AO Branch was to deal with it.

The package of captured documents etc (sent by E on 16 April) had now arrived at F. In fact it only reached the Ic section after having mistakenly first gone to the AO section. This delay led the Ic section 07 officer Lt. Strnad to write a short note on it to the registry NCO that in future all prisoner interrogations would go to him first and not to the AO. On the text alongside the mention of Capt. Blyth, the Ic/AO Branch wrote 'sent direct to Moosburg without our knowledge'.
On 21 April part of F's Ic section provided further translations of several abbreviations contained in the material from the interrogations (Annex 84).

On the same day the Ic/AO Branch of E sent F the originals of the interrogations of the three Greek sailors captured on LS24 who were now clearly in Salonika. These were signed both by the interpreter, who presumably conducted the interrogation, and by Lt. Poliza, who has recently confirmed being responsible for overseeing their interrogation (cf. p. 20). The covering letter was signed not as usual by Lt. Col. Warnstorff (the Ic and head of the Ic/AO Branch) but by his deputy Maj. Hammer (the AO) as Warnstorff was absent on a visit elsewhere. It was initialled by both Lt. Poliza and Lt. Waldheim* (Annex 85). These documents were received by F on the 26 April 1944.

At 1310 hours on 26 April 1944 the Ic/AO Branch in E sent a signal to F saying:

> Further interrogation of the British Alimnia commandos without result. Request decision on whether the prisoners now to be handed over to SD. Suggest Greek sailors be excluded as acting under duress. Apart from the instructions for the captains of the Greek ships and the diary of the English radio operator, no further evidence for communication to Turkey. The English radio operator and the Greek sailor Lisgaris are possible suitable witnesses. Decision requested (Annex 86).

Now that their further interrogation by the Army was seen as valueless, this signal prepared the way for the surrender of the 'commandos' to the SD. It was classified as 'Gkdos'—Geheime Kommandosache (Secret Command matter) and,

* The practice of double initialling is repeated later when again Maj. Hammer signs for Lt. Col. Warnstorff; it is discussed in greater detail later (see chapter 11).

as previously explained, it has been suggested that only the two senior officers in the Ic/AO branch, Warnstorff and Hammer, were authorised to send it (cf. p. 23). On its receipt in F it was clearly seen by the 03 (see the initial in the 03 Box of the F Ic/AO stamp), as well as by von Harling (his initial is to the left of the stamp). But, as it is the copy received by F, the surviving signal provides no indication of who in E ordered its despatch: it bears only the Ic/AO Branch 'signature block'.

The reply from F's Ic/AO Branch was sent the next day, 27 April and said:

1. The British radio operator and the Greek sailor are to be kept under strict guard ready for possible use as witnesses.

2. The other prisoners are to be transferred to the SD for further interrogation if they see fit and subsequent Sonderbehandlung in accordance with the Führerbefehl (Annex 87).

Carpenter, whose diary provided important documentary evidence, was presumably kept as a witness to support any German protests to Turkey.

On 27 and 28 April 1944 von Harling distributed to other Headquarters—OKW, OKH, the Ics in the Air and Naval Südost Headquarters, as well as the Ic with the Bulgarian forces—a report of the party's capture, the intelligence already gathered from the interrogation, the captured SBS insignia and papers previously passed to him by E (Annex 88). This would suggest that he expected that no more information would come from the Army Group E Headquarters and that what there was should therefore be disseminated; any more information obtained by the SD, if they interrogated the prisoners once in their hands, could be passed on later. The fact that, according to Army Group E, the Salonika interrogations had been fruitless, explains why no papers concerning them appear ever to have been sent to Army Group F.

On the 27 or 28 April 1944 von Harling despatched to OKW an analysis of Allied misuse of Turkish waters based on the evidence obtained from the Alimnia party, as well as an analysis of the position with regard to the provisions of International Law concerning breaches of neutrality (Annex 89).

Finally on 29 April Maj. Hammer (presumably again deputising for Warnstorff) signed another letter to F enclosing the carbon copies of the originals of the interrogations (carried out on Rhodes) of the Greek seamen captured with LS24 and the British 'commandos'. Also enclosed were brief summaries of the particulars of the three Greek seamen which had been prepared by the GFP on the island (Annex 90). The covering letter was initialled by both Lt. Poliza and Lt. Waldheim. (These documents had been received by E on 24 April).

On 1 May 1944 F at last received from OKH a copy of the Moosburg report of Capt. Blyth's interrogation, completed there on 16 April 1944 (Annex 91). It was in turn sent on to E by F on 4 May 1944 (Annex 92).

On 3 May 1944, the Ic/AO Branch in F received the package of the original Rhodes interrogations. For some reason this package was booked into the classified document register as an AO item, perhaps because it was signed by the

AO in E (cf Annex 90) but only on 13 May 1944 were copies of this material distributed respectively to the Ics of Naval South and Air South-East Headquarters (Annex 93).

On 22 May 1944, some three and a half weeks after the decision to keep Carpenter and Lisgaris back as potential witnesses, F enquired of the OKW if the two witnesses should continue to be held by High Command South East, Army Group F for possible use or, if not, where they should be sent. The only signature on the surviving copies is that of Lt. Col Hinterseer the AO and von Harling's deputy. This suggests that von Harling was temporarily absent when the signal was actually despatched. (Annex 94). At 1235 hours on 4 June 1944 Gen. Warlimont in OKW replied to von Harling's question:

> As the evidence forwarded is sufficient for presentation to the Turkish Government, according to the Foreign Ministry, the British wireless operator Carpenter and the Greek sailor Lisgaris, captured off Alimnia, are no longer required and are released for Sonderbehandlung in accordance with the Führerbefehl. (Annex 95).

This information was passed by von Harling to E as an order from the OKW:

> By order of OKW/WFst the British radio operator and the Greek sailor Lisgaris, captured off Alimnia, are no longer required and are released for Sonderbehandlung in accordance with the Führerbefehl. (Annex 96).

The F copy of this was distributed internally first to the 07—responsible for the enemy situation in Greece and the Allies—and then for filing in F's Ic/AO Branch's special 'Alimnia file' (cf. p. 105). This signal concludes the material from the Army Group F file.

According to the office stamps on the document the information on the Raiding Forces organisation and recognition signals etc which the Ic/AO Branch in E had passed to the Ia (operations branch) in mid April (cf. p. 52) was re-examined at the end of July 1944 for some reason by the Operations staff of E. This was perhaps because, following further Raiding Forces operations, they wished to re-examine relevant information gleaned from the Alimnia prisoners. It is the only surviving document from E's papers on the Alimnia party. The reason for this would seem to be that, as it passed into the Ia (operations) files, it escaped the careful destruction of such material conducted by E's Ic/AO Branch.

Allied efforts to establish the party's fate: 1944–1946

The British investigations into the fate of the Alimnia party began in 1944.

As already noted, the SBS in the area were soon aware that the party had clashed with the Germans. The British report on Operation Fireater—written in June 1944—concluded that the fate of the patrol was uncertain but that, according to a German report (obviously the Wehrmachtbericht), it was wiped out. Enquiries in the period since the patrol's disappearance had produced somewhat conflicting information. Initial reports said that LS24 had stopped at Calchi and that the Greek crew had spoken with some of the island's inhabitants one of whom had then informed the Germans of the party's arrival. The Germans had then sent two boats to cut the British vessel off and during the ensuing battle the British captain had sabotaged his vessel, the Greek crew were killed and the two British on the boat were captured. A subsequent report that reached the SBS soon after these said that the Greek crew had been captured but were court martialled and shot, while the two British naval crewman had been killed in the fighting and the remainder of the party were prisoners of war.

However on 11 June the Advanced Raiding Forces Headquarters advised the authorities in Cairo that Capt. Blyth was known to be a prisoner of war in Germany (Annex 97). By 17 June 1944 Maj. Sutherland (the SBS Detachment's commander) had received information via a third party that the whole group had since been reported as prisoners of war in Germany. This statement was believed to be based on information from Mrs Blyth who had received a letter from her husband, himself a prisoner of war in Germany. As a result, on 20 June 1944 Headquarters Raiding Forces advised the Officer Commanding RN Coastal Forces at the Beirut base in the Middle East that Blyth had stated in a letter that, amongst others, the naval officer missing at the same time was safe and also a prisoner of war in Germany. Although no names were mentioned, the naval officer was 'probably Lt. Tuckey' (Annex 98). There was clearly some confusion over the actual contents of Capt. Blyth's letter. Mrs Blyth has since confirmed that she had not received a letter from him making these claims about his companions and that he always said he had not seen any of the men of his party again after he left Rhodes (4). The probable explanation is that he actually said he had last seen the men alive and well as prisoners of war (meaning on Rhodes) but that, as he wrote from a prisoner of war camp in Germany, his statement was misinterpreted as meaning he had seen them in Germany. Unfortunately none of his letters to his wife now survive and it is only possible to speculate on the cause of this confusion.

As part of the Services' efforts to trace the men, in August and September 1944 the International Committee of the Red Cross (ICRC) was requested by both the War Office and Admiralty to ask Blyth on their behalf for information on the rest of his party, including the naval personnel.

In October the War Office requested the headquarters in the Middle East to pass on any details they had on the disappearance and fate of Capt. Blyth's party. The SBS headquarters there replied that information had been received from Intelligence sources to the effect that personnel answering their description had been seen as prisoners of war, but no suggestion as to the location of this sighting was given. In November Blyth responded to the ICRC enquiry about Tuckey and said that he had last seen him on the day after his capture (i.e. 8 April 1944). In a further reply in January 1945 he expanded on this and said that, on arrival at the quayside in Rhodes on 7 April, he and Tuckey had been separated from the other ranks whom he did not see again. The two officers were interrogated separately, at Rhodes Town. Blyth saw Tuckey the following morning (8 April) but did not speak to him; this was the last time he saw Tuckey. On the afternoon of 8 April Blyth was flown to Athens. The whole party was uninjured when captured, except for two of the Greek crew who were sent to a hospital on Rhodes. Tuckey was in the best of health when last seen and was being well treated by the Germans.

Blyth then speculated on their fate suggesting that Sub/Lt. Tuckey might have attempted to escape or had been taken to the Greek mainland by sea and met some accident en route (Annex 99).

Despite Capt. Blyth's statements, there was still some confusion over the party's last known whereabouts. In a War Office letter in February 1945, probably before Blyth's letter had reached London, he is said to have stated that he believed the British party were seen on about 16 April 1944 at or near Moosburg Transit Camp (Stalag VIIA in Bavaria, South Germany) where Blyth had been flown soon after his capture. By 24 April 1944 Blyth himself had been moved to an officers' camp (Oflag VIIIF in Czechoslovakia). Subsequently the ICRC stated that they had no evidence that any of the personnel in question had been held as prisoners in the Moosburg Transit Camp. This sequence reflects the errors stemming from the apparent miscomprehension of Blyth's original letter to his wife, discussed earlier.

The War Office pursued the case further and in April 1945 requested the ICRC to approach the German Government on this matter. However, no reply was received from the Germans before their surrender and the end of the War in Europe in May 1945. At about the same time the Middle East Headquarters stated that no new information was available despite repeated efforts on the part of A Force/MI9 which dealt with escapers and evaders.

Blyth had now been liberated and had completed a prisoner of war debrief form. But this added little to the information already available (Annex 100).

On 7 June 1945, subsequent to the Germans' final surrender, the British Military Administration in the Aegean/Dodecanese was asked to make investigations 'on the ground' among the local inhabitants. On 11 July this request was repeated, asking for special efforts to be made on Alimnia and Rhodes. By mid June 1945, the War Office casualty branch had examined the captured German PW records but had found no trace of the men.

The British Combined Services Detailed Interrogation Centre (CSDIC) then reported that enquiries had been made among German service personnel now held as prisoners of war on Rhodes, including members of the Island's intelligence staff, and had revealed that the Army staff who would have been responsible for Allied prisoners in April 1944 had been evacuated to the Greek mainland in late September 1944. One small piece of information was gained however from the German naval intelligence officer who had also been on Rhodes in April 1944. He revealed to CSDIC that German policy was to evacuate British PWs to Piraeus, the port of Athens on the mainland, after a quick operational interrogation. But he could not recall the interrogation of a British naval officer. However the names were obtained of three of the German Army intelligence staff who had been on the island in April 1944 (Lt. Brenner, Lt. Lochner and Sgt. Viebrock) and on 14 September 1945 the War Office requested the Search Bureau (Prisoner of War and Displaced Persons Division) of the British Army's Headquarters in Germany (HQ BAOR), as well as the Casualty Division there, to locate and interrogate these Germans. Initial efforts were clearly unsuccessful as reminders were sent in November 1945, and January and March 1946.

Efforts also continued in the Mediterranean. One of the Greek fishermen (Jouse)—from the boat on which Blyth and the other SBS men tried to escape—was located and interviewed by the British authorities. He told how they helped five British persons, whom he described erroneously as one naval officer, one 'coporal' and three OR's. He said that after their capture and movement to Rhodes, they were joined on the quayside there by three Greek naval sailors and one British sailor, all of whom had been captured separately. Jouse did not see any of the men during his period of capture or after his release (it will be remembered that he was set free after six days) and he had no idea of their fate. Something said by Blyth or the Greeks led to the suggestion at that time that some of the party had tried to escape by swimming to the mainland: but the evidence for this theory is unclear (Annex 101).

The Service authorities had two concerns here: as well as naturally trying to establish the fate of missing men, they also had a responsibility to their next of kin to allow the administration of their personal estates and the finalising of other personal matters to proceed as soon as it appeared that there was little, if any, hope of their survival. An important part in this process was a formal decision by the Service authorities that a missing individual's death should be legally 'presumed'.

As the contemporary records show (Annex 102), the Service authorities were willing to wait until a response had been received from the search for the three Germans from Rhodes. However, by the end of 1945 the Service authorities clearly believed that no further progress was likely to be made despite their continuous efforts. On 19 January 1946 the War Office gave approval for the 'Presumption of death' in the case of Gnr. Jones. In April the naval cases were also dealt with, Sub/Lt. Tuckey and Telegraphist Carpenter being formally recorded as 'Presumed dead' on 20 April 1946, while the 'presumptions' for the three other soldiers (Pte. Evans, Pte. Rice and L/Sgt. Miller) followed on 23 April, 25 April and 27 May 1946 respectively.

With hindsight these decisions may seem premature, but there were many 'missing' servicemen and the Services were trying to deal fairly with all of them and their families. This meant that cases where there seemed no likelihood of the individual's having survived had to be closed. The question of what information should be passed to the next of kin concerning the individual's fate was always a difficult one. An internal letter from the casualties branch (Annex 103) highlights their dilemma. A further complication was the secrecy which at that time still surrounded some aspects of Special Forces and their operations.

Further investigations by Sub/Lt. Tuckey's family

The family of Sub/Lt. Tuckey had been making strenuous efforts to ascertain his fate and were not prepared to accept the lack of firm evidence as to his end. They not only approached the Admiralty but made their own enquiries through personal contacts. Tuckey's brother (Lt. Col. H. L. Tuckey) was serving with the British element of the Control Commission in Germany (CCG) and, therefore, was aware of certain possible avenues of enquiry. In February 1946 the family received a response from a Greek naval officer whom they had approached for help in tracing the Greek seamen with the party. This letter pointed out that:

> The Levant Schooner crews and all commandos in general were considered by the Germans as spies and dealt with as such. It has moreover been revealed at the Nuremberg trial that Hitler had personally given orders for all commandos to be shot (Annex 104).

As part of the search the CCG's Search Bureau made approaches to the United Nations Relief and Rehabilitation Agency (UNRRA). These resulted in the receipt of information that three German servicemen with the names of Lt. Lochner, Lt. Brenner and Sgt. Viebrock had been located in Prisoner of War Camps in France. The CCG Search Bureau now approached the British War Crimes Unit in Germany for help.

As part of its efforts to bring to justice those accused of war crimes, the United Kingdom had established a war crimes investigative organisation primarily under War Office control exercised through the Judge Advocate General's office in London and through the Judge Advocates in the appropriate theatres i.e. BAOR, Italy (also covering Austria and the Balkans), and, for a short while, Norway. This organisation worked in conjunction with other British and Allied bodies concerned with security and counter-intelligence matters, including the relevant parts of the Control Commission. The trial of war criminals, apart from those tried before the International Military Tribunal at Nuremberg (IMT), was the responsibility of the respective zonal authorities in Germany and of individual states elsewhere. In the case of the United Kingdom, trials of war criminals were mainly heard before Military Courts established under a Royal Warrant dated 14 June 1945 (Annex 105).

Once the appropriate British war crimes section considered that there was clear evidence of a crime, it would be taken up by one of the investigating teams and, where suspects were not yet in custody, CROWCASS and the UNWCC (two war crimes bodies*) would be advised of their details and a search would be made for the men among PW in Allied hands. Help was also sought from a British war crimes sub-unit of British service personnel who specialised in tracing suspects and witnesses wanted by the investigating team; these men became known as 'Haystack' teams because of the difficulty in finding individuals amongst millions of prisoners and refugees.

The BAOR War Crimes Section replied to the CCG Search Bureau's approach as follows:

> 1. As you have applied for information to this office it seems probable that you suspect that a war crime has been committed in this case. Before we can however brief a team to investigate this case, we must be satisfied that there is sufficient evidence to support a theory that Sub-Lt. TUCKEY'S disappearance was due to war crimes and not to any ordinary explanation. If you have no evidence in your possession or do not suspect that this officer was the subject of war crimes, then we suggest that you refer the case to the Intelligence Div, CCG (BE), as this office cannot spare members of its small staff to inquire into the mere disappearance of individuals (Annex 106).

* Both CROWCASS and the UNWCC are covered more fully later (cf. p. 102 and 101).

Tuckey's family now prepared as full an account of the Alimnia case as possible (Annex 107) and forwarded this to the War Crimes Section in early November 1946. Satisfied that there was justification for at least an initial investigation of this case, a sub-unit of the war crimes organisation was tasked in December 1946 to interrogate the three Germans. The result (received in February 1947) was that, although the men concerned had the same surnames as those being sought, unfortunately they were clearly not the individuals required.

The War Crimes Group, as it was now called, advised the Tuckey family of the unsuccessful outcome and that:

> It is regretted that no satisfactory result has been achieved and that the disappearance of your brother Sub-Lt. Allan Lane TUCKEY is still unsolved. Should any further information be received by this office steps will be taken for the case to be re-opened pending which the matter must of course remain in abeyance. Although it is realised that this knowledge can be of little consolation, it is the opinion of this office with regard to the facts available that your brother was not a victim of a war crime (Annex 108).

It is impossible to tell what the reasons were for this view, which seemed to discount the possibility that the party had fallen victim to the 'Commando Order' as had been suggested in the summary of the case passed to them. At about the same time the Tuckey family, in a letter to a friend discussing a rather erroneous report that they had received from Greek sources, not only stressed their belief that the party had been shot but mentioned a recently published book by John Lodwick, (a fellow member of the SBS) which discussed the incident*.

This account is especially interesting as, although the existence of the 'Commando Order' was now more widely known, Lodwick suggested that the fact that he and his patrol had survived German captivity, despite causing considerable damage to German supply dumps just before capture, indicated that the Germans were treating British Raiding Forces personnel as prisoners of war. He suggested that the general feeling in SBS circles was that Blyth's party died either in an air crash or in a ship torpedoed by an Allied submarine while en route as prisoners of war from Rhodes to the Greek mainland.

Although the War Crimes team had apparently ceased active investigations in this case, the war crimes 'Haystack' system of circulating the names of individuals wanted for interrogation continued. In August 1947, one of the Germans being sought (H. Viebrock) was located in the American Zone of Germany, and his transfer to the British Zone for interrogation was arranged. This news was relayed to the Tuckey family.

The location of Sgt. Viebrock provided the initial breakthrough as he was able to give the British the first full account of the party's movements on Rhodes and their departure from the island for, he believed, Salonika, since that was the location of the Army Group's Headquarters. Viebrock was also able to provide Lt. Lochner's address and the latter was located and interrogated. He

* John Lodwick, 'The Filibusters'; Methuen, London. 1947

corroborated Viebrock's account and provided in turn an address for a friend of Maj. Kronsbein who, it was appreciated, would be the only one of the Germans so far identified who would know what happened to the party after they left Rhodes. The War Crimes Unit's correspondence suggests that there was still doubt in the investigator's mind as to whether the missing party were in fact the victims of a war crime (Annex 109).

Kronsbein was traced through his friend and his account revealed that the Commander of Crete (Gen. Kleeman) had ordered him to fly the party (minus Blyth) to Salonika where they were met by Lt. Col. Warnstorff the Intelligence Officer of 'Army Group C' (an error for E) (5). The search now switched to locate Gen. Kleeman and Warnstorff (Annex 110).

In spite of the latest news, the Tuckey family appear still to have been 'quite convinced' that the party were shot on Rhodes, a view they communicated to the Foreign Office. At about the same time a private friend of the family, who obviously had personal contacts in the intelligence area, wrote to tell them that the Force 133 (SOE) records could cast no light on the matter beyond that already known. He added that he had passed all the details to his contacts, though he warned that enquiries of this kind often took a long time to resolve (6).

The BAOR war crimes team followed up the leads from Maj. Kronsbein and the information obtained by the Americans in their interrogation of Gen. Kleeman for the British. Kleeman had mentioned Lt. Col. von Harling as another possible source of information and by mid March 1948 he had been located and arrested. At this time another part of the North West Europe War Crimes Group, the Special Air Service War Crimes Investigation Team (SASWCIT) led by Maj. Barkworth, became interested in the case. The SASWCIT had already investigated a number of other cases of SAS personnel executed under the 'Commando Order' in North West Europe and Italy and had had considerable success in bringing the perpetrators to justice. The team was now in the process of investigating the responsibility of individuals in the German High Command for the implementation of the 'Commando Order' and was searching among the German documents with the US Army's war crimes team at Nuremberg. These documents had been selected from captured German archives which by then were held in Washington (Annex 111).

Four documents which seemed to provide a suitable example of the application of the 'Commando Order' were being prepared for use in a war crimes trial known as the 'High Command Trial' before an American Military Tribunal and these came to the SASWCIT's attention in May 1948. (The documents were actually used in court in late June/early July 1948 and the Alimnia Case formed part of the charges against Gen. Warlimont of the OKW who sent the signal ordering the handover of Carpenter and Lisgaris to the SD (Annex 112)). As these documents clearly related to the Alimnia party, the SASWCIT made contact with the other war crimes team which had been dealing with this party's fate, the case having the title with them of the 'Rhodes Case'. The SASWCIT now took over the investigation, presumably because of the team's knowledge of the 'Commando Order' and its implementation.

These documents by no means comprised copies of all the papers concerning the Alimnia party in the surviving German records then in America; only the most relevant documents concerning the 'High Command Trial' had been extracted and sent to Germany (see Chapter 12). Nevertheless, they were sufficient to indicate the intended fate of the party and to identify Lt. Col. von Harling as having been closely involved in the despatch of the signals recorded in these documents. Von Harling's subordinate intelligence officer Capt. Merram was now also arrested. While von Harling was being questioned, the War Crimes Group was still trying to locate Lt. Col. Warnstorff as a possible witness, but the returns from the Prisoner of War Directorate were negative as he was not in UK/US hands.

This investigation was now taking place against the background of the United Kingdom's decision in March 1948 not to commence further war crimes trials before Military Courts after 31 August 1948. (The background to this decision is covered more fully in Annex 113). There was therefore a need for rapid progress with the case. In early August 1948 the CCG advised the Foreign Office that the War Crimes Group expected to place von Harling on trial 'in the very near future' and that one of the charges would concern the 'disposal' of Sub/Lt. Tuckey.

In the event, although this was now the only case being worked on by the SASWCIT (Annex 114), it was not sufficiently far advanced by 15 August 1948 to allow it to be submitted for trial before 1 September. On 23 August 1948 therefore the War Crimes Group formally advised the lawyers of von Harling and Merram that it had now been decided not to prosecute them before a Military War Crimes Court and both were to be transferred to a Civilian Internment Camp (CIC) 'for disposal under the authority of the Intelligence Division 70 Headquarters CCG(BE)' to whom all the papers were being forwarded (7). This was the division which was acting as the focal point for enquiries about the Alimnia party from the Foreign Office.

The order transferring von Harling and Merram to the CIC had stipulated that they were not to be released without the authority of the Intelligence Division CCG (Annex 115). Although there was the implication that some proceedings before a Control Commission Court had not been wholly ruled out, the transfer documents had also stated that neither von Harling nor Merram were of any further War Crimes interest. The Intelligence Division gave orders for von Harling's release on 14 September 1948 on conditions that required him to report to the police any change of address.

The statement by the CCG to the Foreign Office in November 1948 that, as von Harling had not been put on trial by the War Crimes Group he had been released, sparked off a further spate of correspondence at the end of the year. Checks in the CCG found that the Alimnia Report compiled by Barkworth had not been received. (In fact Barkworth had not submitted it for forwarding until October 1948 by which time von Harling had already been released). The CCG's own internal enquiries further showed that the lack of any clear intelligence interest in von Harling or the Tuckey case (which was seen as a war crimes matter) lay behind the decision of the Intelligence Division of the CCG to permit von Harling's release; as the Intelligence Division noted, it had merely been acting as a 'go-between' for the FCO and the War Crimes organisation in Germany

(Annex 116). The Intelligence Division's summary of the situation noted that 'much time has been wasted by various officers since July '45 in chasing shadows. The word "wasted" is used advisedly because no information has resulted and false hopes have been kept alive by reporting every incidental chimera' (Annex 117).

Unfortunately the main SASWCIT report was apparently lost in transit and was not received by the CCG, which made a resolution of the situation difficult. However early in January 1949 Barkworth responded to the CCG Intelligence Division's request for help and provided a summary of the case from memory. This identified von Harling as the individual who 'gave instructions for the liquidation of the prisoners'. Barkworth felt that further investigations would be necessary. These should include the Salonika SD and the Abwehr unit attached to the Army Group, presumably to try and identify who carried out the subsequent executions. Barkworth considered that, of the individuals from Army Group E's Headquarters, the Ic (Lt. Col. Warnstorff) and the AO (Maj. Hammer) might be able to provide useful information. Of course unsuccessful attempts had already been made to trace Warnstorff who, like Hammer, had apparently not fallen into British hands at the end of the war. Barkworth's investigations into other 'Commando Order' cases (in France) also led him to suggest that the SD might have refused actually to execute the prisoners themselves, forcing this task on the Abwehr or even troops from the Army Group HQ itself. Barkworth also pointed out that von Harling had refused to answer any questions on the subject (Annex 118). The outline of the defence planned by von Harling was that he was merely a channel for orders (Annex 119).

In fact at the end of 1947 when Gen. Kleeman was being asked by the Allies about the fate of the Alimnia party, he contacted von Harling in case he could throw any light on the subject. The latter's reply claimed that at least two individuals from the party, one a 'Capt. Hopkins' who was wounded, were saved from Sonderbehandlung by von Harling's intervention (8). Clearly these men were not from the Alimnia party. No trace has been found of this 'Capt. Hopkins' and von Harling's claims sit somewhat uneasily alongside the documentary evidence of his activities in connection with the 'Commando Order'. Significantly there is no mention by his lawyer of this 'evidence' of his frustration of the requirements of the 'Commando Order' in the war crimes papers.

The Foreign Office were still pressing the CCG for a comprehensive answer (Annex 120) and also asking the War Office for any information they had in order to advise Sub/Lt. Tuckey's relatives of the party's fate (Annex 121).

In response the CCG Intelligence Division discussed the case with their Legal Division to see if a case could be brought under their auspices. In May 1949 the CCG provided the Foreign Office with a summary of the situation. Even after receiving Barkworth's summary of his findings there was it seems insufficient evidence to prosecute von Harling (Annex 122).

In the autumn of 1950 the Tuckey family, having heard nothing since the end of 1948, again approached the Foreign Office who, after acknowledging the enquiry (Annex 123), in due course sent them a resume of the available information on the fate of the party and the authorities' inability to produce a sustainable case against any individual (Annex 124). There the matter rested and unfortunately there seems by that date to have been no mechanism by which the different Government Departments involved considered the question of informing the next of kin of the other members of the Alimnia party of the information by then available.

Summary of knowledge of the fate of the party

It appears that no real consideration was given to the possibility that, following their capture, the Alimnia party might have been executed by the Germans until the further investigations instigated in 1947 as a result of the Tuckey family's refusal to accept an incomplete answer led to the involvement of the British war crimes organisation. As a result of these further investigations, which ceased in 1949, all that could be deduced was that the party, with the exception of Capt. Blyth, had been moved to Salonika and that instructions had been given for their transfer to the SD for Sonderbehandlung.

Subsequent recent investigations have revealed that another Greek (now deceased) held prisoner by the Germans is reported to have said that she saw Lisgaris, one of the Greek sailors from the LS24, in one of the German prisons in Athens (9). As already noted, Lisgaris was held back with Carpenter when the rest of the group were presumably released to the SD in April 1944. It is possible that, as these two men were being held as potential witnesses to support official complaints by the Germans to the Turkish authorities, they were sent to Athens, the location of the German politico/military headquarters for Greece. It seems less likely that the other members of the party would have been moved south to Athens.

Unfortunately, unlike those civilian individuals who were executed in reprisals by the Germans and whose names were on occasion revealed in order to increase the 'deterrent' effect, Allied personnel who were executed under the 'Commando Order' were usually treated in the same way as others handled under the system known as 'Nacht und Nebel' (literally 'night and fog'). This kept only very limited records and was designed to hide all traces of its victims' existence and eventual fate. It may even be that, as happened to some British 'commandos' from other theatres, the party was taken to Germany where their secret disposal was more easily achieved.

It is greatly regretted that, even after such detailed research, this Review has been unable to obtain any new concrete evidence as to the fate of the British members of the Alimnia party. The date and the place of their presumed execution are still unknown. The German agency most probably involved, the SD, was very thorough in its destruction of its documents before the end of the war. Of the individuals who served in the area, the key men in the GFP and SD, as well as the AO of Army Group E, are all dead. Of the surviving German servicemen from the area, none was in a position to know the full picture and none traced has been able to provide any new evidence concerning the men's fate.

CHAPTER 7: References

(1) Thames Television.

(2) MOD Archives.

(3) Correspondence between Alexander MacLeod Esq and Andrew Tuckey Esq.

(4) MOD correspondence and discussion with Mrs Blyth.

(5) MOD Archives.

(6) Papers of A. Tuckey Esq.

(7) MOD Archives.

(8) Correspondence with Gerald Fleming Esq.

(9) Correspondence with Mario Modiano Esq.

Chapter 8: The Yannina Case

This section concerns the party of Allied servicemen called here the 'Yannina party' which consisted of:

Capt. J. W. S. Hamilton, Force 133, (Argyll & Sutherland Highlanders).

Capt. C. R. Bluett, Raiding Support Regiment (RSR), (Union Defence Force).

Pte. A. E. Davies, RSR, (Royal Armoured Corps).

Gnr. L. T. Bennett, RSR, (Royal Artillery).

All these men survived the war. The allegations against the then Lt. Waldheim in connection with this case are that he was personally involved in their interrogation, or in the organisation and control of matters relating to their interrogation and treatment whilst in German hands in Salonika and that he was therefore responsible for any ill-treatment suffered by them during this captivity.

In the autumn of 1943 it was decided to create a unit to provide heavy fire support for special operations in the Balkans, whether in support of Allied regular raiding forces or of the partisans. This unit was designated the Raiding Support Regiment (RSR) and was established in October 1943. It consisted of a Headquarters and five batteries, respectively one of Mountain Guns, one of Anti-Tank Weapons, one of Anti-Aircraft Guns, one of Medium Machine Guns, and one of Mortars. The troops for this unit were all volunteers for special operations, but the unit was part of the British Army and its members were soldiers operating in uniform as part of a formally organised military body.

Some elements of the Regiment were committed on operations in January 1944 after only initial training, while the remainder of the unit completed their training. Later in the year 112 men from elements of the RSR were infiltrated into Greece by sea as part of Operation Glasshouse, having left Italy on or about 22 April 1944 on a landing craft. The men comprised No. 2 Troop A Battery, less No. 4 Section, and No. 3 Troop B Battery, less No. 2 Section. The aim of the operation was to rendezvous on the Greek coast with the partisans who would bring mules and ponies to carry the heavy weapons (mortars and machine guns). The combined RSR and partisan party would then move to its planned area of operations inland.

Having met the partisan force and the British officers from the Allied Military Mission (Maj. R. R. Prentice and Capt. J. W. S. Hamilton) who acted as guides and liaison officers, the combined force with its convoy of some 200 mules and ponies made its way across country towards its planned area of operations in Pendalaphon. The route the convoy was to take meant that it had at some point to cross main roads which, although few, were a hazard because naturally the Germans sought to control them if nothing more.

As the force neared the main road to Yannina there was, unknown to them, a considerably enhanced German presence in the area. On the previous night (4 May 1944) three small German strongpoints on the road had been attacked, captured and set on fire by the partisans. According to German records, at 1900 hours on 5 May 1944 the III Battalion 724 Light Infantry Regiment was ordered by its Corps (XXII (Geb.) A.K.) to send a reinforced company to the area to see if anything could be discovered of the German personnel and to take steps to resecure the area. These troops moved up the road sweeping about 1 km to the left and right of it. The strongpoint positions were found to be totally destroyed by fire and no equipment was left, suggesting that they had been plundered before burning. There was no evidence of any real defence at the positions: the local inhabitants said that about midnight there had been heavy machine gun and rifle fire after which the strongpoints were set on fire. In all, four Germans and a number of Greek auxiliaries were missing.

After the clearance operation the Germans set up four watch posts along the road, while the Command Post had the integral artillery platoon of 75 mm Infantry Guns (IG) under command. In the dawn light of 6 May 1944 the Germans saw a large column of armed partisans with some 60 mules about 1 km south of Asprangeloi: it was moving north. The column was immediately taken under artillery fire from the IG platoon, with the result that it split up. The partisans were seen to disperse in flight north-east towards Asprangeloi and on reaching a crest passed out of sight. The Germans immediately sent one platoon of II Company in pursuit. The climb took about one hour so that the partisans had a good lead and had time to get a large number of the mules away. The German report further stated that as their troops reached the top of the slope there was a short firefight with a small party of British soldiers.

Capt. Bluett, who was in charge of No 2 Troop, had ordered the rest of the Allied force in the vicinity to move on as fast as possible while he with Capt. Hamilton, Pte. Davies and Pte. Bennett stayed to round up some stray mules, five of whom had shed their loads which included the medical equipment and a radio set.

Suddenly surrounded by superior numbers of German troops the British party was captured. Pte. Davies appears to have received a slight wound to his ankle but, though there have beeen recent suggestions (made during interviews for the Thames Television programme) that Capt. Hamilton was wounded in the head during this action, this is not supported by the contemporary evidence from British and German sources nor by his family's recollections: any such wound must therefore have been insignificant. Also the German documents—normally meticulous in reporting casualty and prisoner information—make no reference to the capture of any Greek partisans, something also recently mentioned by a member of the British party* (1).

The German unit had clearly reported the basic details of these events to XXII (Geb.) AK by signal, as at 1530 hours on 6 May 1944 the Corps itself sent a 'contact report' (Sofortmeldung) to the Army Group E Headquarters for the operations staff and the intelligence branch. This stated that in the follow up to the artillery fire the German troops had captured the four British prisoners and

* However British records mention a member of the Cyprus Regiment (Pte. Tsappis) who had been captured in 1941 after the campaign in Greece but had escaped and later joined the AMM as a helper, probably as a muleteer. He was recorded as 'missing' on about the 7 May 1944. There are no references in German or other British records to the capture of any other British personnel at this time. It is therefore possible that he was either killed during this German anti-partisan operation or captured and treated as a Greek partisan. There is no other information on his fate.

twenty to thirty mules with ammunition, mines, explosives, weapons and one radio; a further 10 mules had been killed, only a few escaping (Annex 125). In its subsequent written report to the Corps the German unit reported that the remainder of the enemy had escaped, blood trails suggesting large numbers of wounded. There is a reference to one enemy dead in the area. Ten mules had been killed or so badly wounded by the artillery fire that they had to be destroyed; eighteen others had been captured. A subsequent reconnaissance towards the north-east had revealed no further trace of the enemy.

After their capture the four Britons were taken to Yannina where they were questioned and condemned to death for operating with partisans. One of the men (Pte. Davies) has recently recounted to Thames Television that, when told by the Germans that he was going to be shot on the night of 7/8 May, this was no more than he had expected from the tales that he had heard before (2).

On the 6 May 1944 XXII (Geb.) A. K. signalled to Feldgendarmerie (Military Police) Troop 422 that:

> The captured Britons Capt. Bluett, Capt. Hamilton, Pte. Davies and Pte. Bennett are to be transported to the Ic Branch of Army Group E at Salonika. As agreed in the telephone conversation with Army Group E, Military Police Troop 422 to move them to Larissa where they are to be handed over to the Railway officer who will make arrangements for them to be moved to Salonika by the next available train (Annex 126).

The results of the preliminary interrogation and the analysis of the captured papers and equipment were sent by letter to E on 6 May 1944 at the same time as the prisoners were forwarded to E. This letter gave full personal details of the four prisoners and added the comment of Capt. Bluett that he had a three day march behind him. The letter also said that from the captured papers it was probable that there were more British soldiers—possibly paratroopers—with the column but the prisoners refused to admit this. The Britons also refused any further information so that it could not be established from where they had come and where they were going. But Greek correspondence captured on one of the mules suggested that the convoy was carrying ammunition and weapons from the coast of South Albania to the interior. This view was supported by the captured documents of the partisan 'IX Division' which was considered to be the column's probable destination (Annex 127).

The Corps daily operational report, sent later in the day to Army Group E, merely repeated the basic outline of the incident as given at the conclusion of the original report sent the morning before (Annex 128). The basic details, including the capture of four Britons, were passed by E to F in the Operations Group daily report sent at 1325 hours 7 May 1944 (Annex 129). Subsequent German documents merely included details of the enemy casualties and captured equipment in their 'monthly' returns of such information.

The British forces in Greece were immediately aware of the loss of the men and the party's capture was reported to the Force 133 Headquarters by signal on 7 May 1944. Claims by some Greeks that the convoy's route had been betrayed are not supported by the contemporary evidence.

The account of the party's subsequent experience is drawn largely from British sources, both from contemporary documents and recent testimony for the Thames Television programme. According to Capt. Bluett the group were moved by the Feldgendarmerie by road to Trikkala and then by train to Salonika. The duration of the move was one day by road with an overnight stop and another one full day by rail (3).

When the party arrived in Salonika, they were placed in what they later reported to be 'Gestapo' prison No 518 or 918. During the Austrian Commission's discussions, Lt. Col. Warnstorff said there were no Gestapo in Salonika (4). It is accepted that, as is clear from the contemporary documents, this is correct and it was indeed the GFP prison not a Gestapo prison. However, all the references to this prison by these British servicemen in their early post-war reports are to 'Gestapo' and never to the GFP.

In his official post-liberation debrief and statements Capt. Bluett said only that he was kept in close confinement in a dark cell 8′ × 8′ for four weeks until he was taken to a ground floor cell where he remained until 20 August. He made no mention of any interrogations.

In his testimony for the Thames Television programme, Capt. Bluett has stated that at his first interrogation two SS men, a prison guard and an interpreter in Wehrmacht uniform (probably a private) were present; the SS men hit him with rubber truncheons. After 30 minutes of interrogation he was returned to his cell. He says he was moved from the cell to another on the first floor next to an interrogation room. A second interrogation took place three weeks later. With a group of other prisoners, including civilians, he was taken to a quadrangle at the back of the building and placed before a Wehrmacht firing squad which fired, even if only at selected individuals, as at least one of the group—a civilian—was hit. Capt. Bluett was then returned to his cell for questioning and was again beaten by the same two SS men who accompanied the 'Gestapo' prison guard and the Wehrmacht interpreter.

The beating was halted by the arrival of an officer who entered the cell behind him and spoke in German in a quiet civilized voice to the other Germans. After the officer left he was returned to his cell. Although he could not see the officer's face Capt. Bluett said that 'peripheral vision' enabled him to register that the man was slim and at least 6 feet tall. (5)

Capt. Bluett in his immediate post-war debrief mentioned that, whilst in the prison, Capt. Hamilton, who spoke Greek and German, talked with a Greek through the bars of his cell. The Greek was Dr Zaminis, a political prisoner condemned to death. He arranged that, if Bluett and Hamilton could get out of their cells, he could then get them out of Salonika. Two attempts were made but on each occasion they were discovered before the plan was brought to a successful conclusion.

None of the above information about interrogations was given in Capt. Bluett's early post war statements. In these he described how after a couple of weeks in the prison he was taken before Uffz Stoffberg, the NCO believed to be in immediate charge of the prison, for refusing to stand to attention when his cell door was opened, and he was threatened with flogging. At the same time his efforts to escape by picking the bolts out of the cell door were discovered and he was in consequence moved to a completely dark room for about five weeks.

In his immediate post-liberation debrief Capt. Bluett described the food as half a pint of cabbage water and a slice of bread a day; the sanitary arrangements were a bucket in the cell; vermin abounded. Repeated requests to see an officer and the Red Cross were refused. On 15 July he collapsed but was denied medical treatment until 17 July when he was taken to an Italian prisoner of war hospital in Salonika and was treated by an Italian doctor. Pte. Bennett collapsed in a similar manner and later entered the same hospital. The implication is that both he and Pte. Bennett collapsed as a result of inadequate food and poor conditions. However, in an affidavit he swore in 1946 for the war crimes investigation, Bluett expanded on these aspects of his captivity and said that on about the 15th July 1944, as a result of a guard kicking over his cabbage soup, he went for the guard in a rush, took him to the stone floor and was battering his head on the stone floor when he was tackled by others and badly beaten up. As a result Capt. Bluett was semi-conscious for two days and on the fourth day (c 19 or 20 July) was taken to an Italian PW hospital in an old school on the main square near the station. He was refused contact with the Red Cross until one day a German NCO—against orders—brought representatives of the International Red Cross to see him.

The post-liberation debrief adds the following further information. On about the 29 July 1944 Capt. Bluett was taken from the hospital to the Wehrmacht Detention Barracks in Salonika where he was told he was to be shot. A fellow prisoner told him that an American Captain from Albania had been removed two days after Bluett's arrival and shot. Capt. Bluett remained in the condemned cell until 20 August 1944 when he was put on a train at Salonika for Germany. At the station he met Capt. Hamilton and Capt. MacGregor (from another Force 133 Mission who had been captured near Athens—see Chapter 10e).

En route to Germany two further unsuccessful attempts were made to liberate the men by the Allied escape organisation (MI9) and the partisans. Bluett arrived at an ordinary prisoner of war camp (Stalag VIIA) on 6 September 1944 and remained there until liberated at the end of the war.

The other men in the party also provided some information of their captivity. In Pte. Davies' initial post-war statement he mentioned personal interrogation, the use of stool pigeons and solitary confinement, and being moved to an 'Italian work camp' after about three and half months in captivity. But he provided no further details for that period. He added that he left the 'Gestapo' prison on 7 August 1944 and eventually ended up in Stalag XIA.

Davies' recent accounts for the Thames Television programme are much fuller. He stated that he was first in a cell on what would seem to have been the first floor of the prison. He said that the guards' uniforms were black or dark, not the grey-green of the Wehrmacht which he said was worn by a soldier who brought his rations to his cell. After two days he was taken from his cell to a room containing three German officers whose uniforms were 'dark'; they were all less than thirty years old and all spoke English, one much better than the others as he corrected some of their mistakes. The questioning lasted about an hour, but there was no pressure to answer the questions and no threats were made. A week or so later three different officers interrogated him. They said they had been sent specially from Berlin. This interrogation also lasted about an hour and was repeated about a week later by the same officers. Shortly after this, a civilian who spoke good English was put into his cell for four or five days and he tried to encourage Davies to talk but without success. He was not physically ill-treated in the prison but heard sounds of beatings and saw other prisoners—civilians—who had been ill-treated. He mentions that the Greek civilian who delivered his soup slipped him a piece of paper with a pencil asking for his Name, Rank and Number, which he presumed were passed to the Red Cross. Pte. Davies mentioned in this recent statement that Capt. Bluett also sent him a message in the same way. (6)

After about three and a half months in prison Pte. Davies was moved to an Italian work camp in Salonika where he remained for about a week. While there he was visited by Red Cross representatives who said that the Germans, furious that the prisoners' existence had become known to the Red Cross, had threatened to arrest the Red Cross officials and had demanded that they tell them how they had heard of the prisoners. After this short stay in the camp, he, Bennett and two American prisoners were taken to the railway sidings just outside Salonika and kept in a cattle truck for two to three days while it was shunted up and down until a complete train had been formed. The journey to Germany took about two weeks, starting around September–October 1944. The food en route was good: the German guards took them into the German forces' canteens to eat with them.

Pte. Bennett's early post war liberation debrief is the least full, mentioning only a period of forty days solitary confinement, thirteen days in a dark cell, all in the 'Gestapo' prison, Salonika.

Capt. Hamilton's accounts, given to the authorities soon after the war, were not very detailed. They make no mention of illegal treatment, apart from his being in solitary confinement until 18 September 1944, charged with suspected espionage. He noted that:

> The other inmates of the prison, many of whom were women hostages, were in most cases treated far worse than us, and some were tortured . . . . Stoffberg was in charge although his senior officers—an Oberfeldwebel, a Sonderführer, a Lieutenant and a Captain used to visit the gaol periodically from Gestapo Headquarters. I was interrogated by the Captain and Sonderführer.

These interrogations were, according to information from his family and ex-colleagues, quite numerous and included one by officers from Berlin (7).

In his post-war statement he mentioned that he made contact with a fellow prisoner, a Greek doctor, who apparently got a note out in the pig swill to Greek friends who then notified the Red Cross of the existence of the British prisoners. Hamilton was, according to family testimony, also twice taken outside and thought he was to be shot. Any such treatment was probably intended to increase the psychological pressure on him and make him less resistant to questioning.

On the question of the notification to the Red Cross of the prisoners' existence, the claim has been made that this was the result of the actions of German servicemen. In an unbroadcast interview during the initial research for the Thames Television programme one German NCO (from the Ic/AO Branch of Army Group E) freely volunteered the information that he had participated in the interrogation of two British officers in Salonika.

One was Scottish in a kilt and the other was South African: these are almost certainly Hamilton and Bluett. He claimed that not only were the interrogations conducted in a friendly, civilised manner without violence or threats of violence but that he and his colleague, who spoke good English and actually asked the questions, recommended to Lt. Col. Warnstorff that the men be taken to hospital where they would be looked after and also become known to the Red Cross, thus ensuring their survival. He claimed that this recommendation was agreed to and implemented (8).

Whatever the reason, both Capt. Bluett and Gnr. Bennett had come to the attention of the Red Cross by July 1944 (Annex 130) and all four men were in due course moved to normal prisoner of war camps in Germany where they remained until the end of the war.

Following their return to the United Kingdom in 1945 from their German prisoner of war camps, at least three of the party (Capt. Bluett, Pte. Davies and Gnr. Bennett) were debriefed by completing the standard ex-prisoner of war form, although Bennett's basic debrief form has not survived (Annexes 131, 132). However Capt. Bluett and Gnr. Bennett also completed 'Form Q' which provided details of alleged war crimes committed against them (Annex 133) and a war crimes case was opened. Capt. Hamilton was contacted and he provided the war crimes investigators with the information mentioned earlier (Annex 134). Capt. Bluett, who had by now returned to South Africa, was also contacted and he provided an affidavit setting out his experiences in greater detail (Annex 135). These papers provided evidence of illegal acts in that the prisoners of war were subjected to:

a. unjustified use of solitary confinement.

b. inadequate food.

c lack of exercise and fresh air.

d. insanitary conditions.

Further possible charges were that they had been told that they had been condemned to death for aiding the partisans; that Capt. Bluett had been threatened with a flogging; and that he had been assaulted. It was considered that Bluett's attack on the guard did not justify the treatment he received.

The men could identify only one of the perpetrators: this was Unteroffizier Paul Stoffberg who was apparently in charge of the prison and who, Capt. Hamilton had been told by the outside Wehrmacht guards, was 'attached to the Gestapo' as were, he thought, the other three members of the permanent staff of the prison (Annex 136). Stoffberg's senior officers—stated by Hamilton to be an

Oberfeldwebel, a Sonderführer, a Lieutenant and a Captain—used to visit the prison occasionally from 'Gestapo' Headquarters. Of these the Captain and Sonderführer had interrogated Hamilton. However, until positive identifications were obtained, no further action could be taken against them. A 'Wanted' report was circulated through the Allied war crimes system for Stoffberg but he was apparently never traced and the case remained untried (Annex 137).

Although, as mentioned in Chapter 4, the GFP in Salonika were to some extent answerable to the Ic of Army Group E, with the AO taking care of day to day matters of deployment etc. there is no evidence that either of these two were considered to be responsible for the actions of the GFP.

CHAPTER 8: References

(1) Thames Television.

(2) Thames Television.

(3) Thames Television.

(4) Austrian Commission.

(5) Thames Television.

(6) Thames Television: unbroadcast interview.

(7) Correspondence with MOD.

(8) Thames Television: unbroadcast interview and correspondence with MOD.

Chapter 9: The Calino Case

This section concerns the fate of the SBS party, called here the 'Calino party', which consisted of:

Sgt. J. Dryden, Royal Artillery.
Pte W. O. Fishwick, East Yorkshire Regt.
Pte J. Doughty, Royal Army Medical Corps (American citizen).

Of these men, both Sgt. Dryden and Pte. Doughty survived the war; Pte. Fishwick died of wounds soon after capture.

The allegations against the then Lt. Waldheim in this case are that he was personally responsible for the interrogation and general treatment of these men whilst prisoners in German hands, and that he was involved in the decision and perhaps personally gave the order that Sgt. Dryden would be handed to the SD for Sonderbehandlung.

Early in June 1944 a reconnaissance mission from the SBS was sent to the island of Calino which it was believed had been heavily reinforced by the Germans following a British raid in April. A ten man patrol was landed and established the presence of a strong German force of at least sixty men in Vathi Bay, an area previously unoccupied. On 8 June 1944 the SBS party was approached by two German soldiers accompanied by a Greek boy who had apparently identified the party's hiding place. The British patrol fired on the Germans, one of whom was killed: the other is stated by British reports to have fallen over a cliff in his efforts to escape but the German records do not report his death or injury, and state that the British forces consisted of three 'commandos'. The British party then withdrew from the island.

It was now decided by the SBS to attack Calino in force. A joint party of fifteen men from the Greek Sacred Squadron and ten men from 'M' Detachment of the SBS under Sgt. J. Dryden, as well as a Greek-speaking British liaison officer, were landed on the island at the end of June.

To carry out the attack on the Vathi Bay area the force split into three patrols and by 2200 hours on the 1 July 1944 these were ready in position and the area had been isolated by cutting all the telephone lines. At about 2200 hours the first shot was fired by the SBS patrol to kill a German sentry guarding a key point. The SBS got into the German troops' sleeping quarters which they attacked. One Greek patrol attacking the same target but from another direction was held up by accurate enemy fire and wire obstacles, while a second Greek patrol engaged the target with its longer range weapons and succeeded in setting the target area on fire.

Although the attackers now believed that the Germans in the target area were dead, news of the attack had apparently been passed to the island's command post almost as soon as the first shots were fired. German records show that at 2225 hours the attack had been reported and the whole island had been placed on alert. Other German positions took up the fight and the area was illuminated by flares. A very heavy barrage of mortar fire came down around the German billets while other German troops approached the area. The Allied force decided to withdraw but during this phase a mortar bomb burst and wounded three of the SBS men (Sgt. Dryden, Pte. Fishwick and Pte. Jackson). The last of these managed to make his way to safety but Sgt. Dryden had been given a morphine injection following his wounding and was too comatose to move. Pte. Fishwick was more seriously wounded. Pte. Doughty, an American serving as a medical orderly with the SBS, decided to stay with the wounded men and the party were concealed in a nearby Greek house for the night. When it became clear the next morning that neither wounded man was fit enough to walk, it was decided by the party and the local inhabitants that they should surrender to the Germans before their discovery placed the lives of the villagers at risk.

Before noon on 2 July 1944 the local German commander was able to provide his superiors with a more detailed report of the affair. This recorded that the attack was a 'commando' operation and noted the wounding of the strongpoint commander (but no further German casualties) as well as the capture of 'three British soldiers (one severely wounded, one lightly wounded), who were transported by Assault boat to the island of Leros (Annex 138). By 1130 hours Doughty had been initially identified as an American medical orderly (based on his own testimony). The discrepancy between the claims of the British for the casualties inflicted on the enemy and the losses recorded by the Germans serves to highlight the inevitable confusion that attends such operations and the difficulty of establishing a full picture from only one source. As the German reports were for official internal use, it is unlikely that any of their own casualties were deliberately concealed from the Germans' higher commands.

The records of Army Group E's Headquarters merely record the bare details of the attack in the War Diary for the afternoon of 2 July 1944 and in the evening Ic/AO Branch's report (Annexes 139 and 140). The Army Group E Headquarters' reports for 3 July 1944 to the High Command South East, Army Group F, merely added the further details on the strength of the party and the items captured in the German 'follow-up' as reported to E by Commander Eastern-Aegean late on 2 July 1944 (Annexes 141 and 142).

According to contemporary records the Allied prisoners had apparently been separated before being moved to Leros, Pte. Doughty being kept apart from the two wounded men who believed that he was still being held on Calino. During the boat trip to Leros, Doughty was questioned by a German officer about the party's mission. On Leros he was interrogated again in the afternoon of 2 July 1944. The German report of the latter interrogation shows that Doughty avoided giving any significant information relating to the operation and that he was warned that he might be treated as an ordinary soldier rather than as a medical orderly as he had no proof of his identity. Doughty was then flown to Rhodes where he remained for a further period of perhaps two days during which time he seems to have been interrogated again. This time he was apparently reluctant to discuss anything, believing, the Germans speculated, that he felt he had said too much during his interrogation on Leros.

As there are apparently no records of any contemporary American debriefing of Doughty after the war, the only further source of information about him is his recent testimony, primarily that for the Thames Television programme. This states that he thinks he was not separated from the other two men until their arrival at Leros when the wounded prisoners were taken to the hospital. (1)

Sgt. Dryden and Pte. Fishwick were moved on 5 July 1944 from Leros to the German Air Force hospital at Piraeus near Athens. Although Pte. Fishwick received medical attention, including a blood transfusion for which Sgt Dryden was apparently compelled to give some blood although he was himself wounded, Pte. Fishwick died of his wounds on 7 July 1944. His death was properly recorded (Annex 143) and reported to the British through the normal channels. Sgt. Dryden's wounds resulted in one of his toes being amputated.

Although, according to his post-war debrief, Sgt. Dryden believed that he was interrogated by a German officer and by two Greek civilians (who claimed to be from the Red Cross) on the same day that Pte. Fishwick died (i.e. 7 July), the German records indicate that his interrogation took place on the 11 July 1944. During this interrogation he deliberately gave the false name of 'Smith' in response to demands for the identity of the officer in command of the raiding party. There is no evidence of any physical violence having been used against Dryden, although he was told by the German officer that he would be shot the next morning. In fact he was transferred to the Averoff prison in Athens and was placed in solitary confinement.

Meanwhile, according to his recent testimony Pte. Doughty had been flown to Athens from Rhodes and thence taken by train to Salonika where he was placed in solitary confinement in one of the prisons in the town. Shortly after his arrival, either in the afternoon of the same day or on the next day, he was interrogated by a German who he believed was an officer who spoke very good English. The interrogation lasted for about an hour but Doughty could recall few details of this man's appearance (2).

The German records of this interrogation, which seems to have taken place on the 17 July 1944 are signed 'F d R' by Wollschläger, a Sonderführer G and a member of the Army Group E Ic section subordinate to Lt. Poliza. Other German colleagues from Army Group E's Headquarters have commented on his good command of English and his role in the interrogation of English-speaking prisoners (cf. p. 20).

A covering note (including a brief assessment of the likely course of the Allied raid on Calino, based on all the interrogations of the prisoners) was initialled by Waldheim, and therefore probably drafted by him, and despatched with the detailed interrogation reports of Sgt. Dryden and Pte. Doughty to High Command South-East Army Group F on 18 July 1944. The covering note records that Doughty, as a medical orderly, having carried no weapons and taken no part in the fighting, had been transferred to the PW Transit Camp in Salonika on 17 July for onward transportation to a PW Camp in Germany. It also stated that Sgt. Dryden would be passed to the SD in accordance with the Führerbefehl (Annex 144).

Doughty's presence in German hands was recorded by the Red Cross in Salonika on 21 July 1944 (Annex 145). During his captivity in Salonika Doughty heard that five or six other British soldiers were also in the prison building and he was transported along with them to Germany when he moved there early in September 1944. Although he cannot now recall with precision, a Cpl. Lumb (with whom he became friendly in the camp in Germany) may have been one of these men (see Chapter 10. Sec. g) (3).

The threatened handover of Sgt. Dryden to the SD did not materialize. He remained in the Averoff Prison in Athens for at least ten weeks. Although usually in solitary confinement, during this period he was allowed to exercise in the prison courtyard and on these occasions he saw several other British prisoners (Capt. Lodwick, Sgt. Nixon, Sgt. O'Neill and Pte. Turton (cf Chapter 10)). At the end of this period of about ten weeks captivity, he was taken to what he described as the 'Gestapo' headquarters in Athens where he remained for about a week. After this Sgt. Dryden was moved to the PW transit camp in Athens and thence to Dulag 185, the prisoner of war transit camp in Salonika, where he remained for some further weeks together with several RAF personnel. His presence in the Salonika Camp was known to the Red Cross in Salonika by 6 October 1944 shortly after his arrival there (Annex 146). There is no evidence that he was interrogated during his stay in Salonika. Finally, with the German withdrawal northwards in October 1944, he was moved with two other British servicemen to Yugoslavia. While being marched to Sarajevo he escaped at night and, having made contact with the partisans, reached the Allied Military Mission and was eventually repatriated to Italy.

There is no evidence that Sgt. Dryden made any charges against the Germans for his treatment whilst in captivity although he was in contact with the British war crimes investigators to help with the case of another prisoner whom he had met whilst in captivity in Athens (cf. p. 90) (Annex 147).

During the American examination of the captured German army papers, the report initialled by Waldheim was noted by the American war crimes investigators as identifying a possible breach of the laws of war in handing over Dryden to the SD. However the records show that the individuals recorded by the American war crimes investigators as being responsible and liable for this proposed breach of the law were the Commanding Generals of Army Groups F & E, and the Chief of Staff of Army Group F. There was no mention of Lt. Waldheim as a potential accused either by name or position (Annex 148).

CHAPTER 9: References

(1) Thames Television.

(2) Thames Television.

(3) Thames Television: unbroadcast interview.

Chapter 10: Other cases concerning British Special Forces personnel and certain non-Special Forces personnel

The following cases concern all other British Special Forces personnel who have been identified as having fallen into German hands in the relevant area of the Balkans during the period under review. It also includes those non-Special Forces cases which are considered necessary to the Report either because they have specifically been brought to the attention of the Ministry of Defence (usually with the suggestion of some illegal involvement of the then Lt. Waldheim) or in one case, that at (m), because the identified individual lost his life while a prisoner whilst in contact with Special Forces personnel.

The cases are considered in chronological order.

a. First Levitha Party.

b. Second Levitha Party.

c. The Leros Party.

d. First Force 133 Party Greece.

e. Second Force 133 Party Greece.

f. Force 133 Individual Greece.

g. RSR/Force 133 Party Greece.

h. SBS Party Crete.

i. RSR Party Greece.

j. Commando/Naval Party Sirina.

k. RSR Individual Greece.

l. Force 133 Individual Crete.

m. Individual Evader Crete/Greece.

n. The Laterina Case.

During the very fluid operations in the Aegean in the Autumn of 1943, following the Italian surrender, both the Allies and Germans captured numbers of each other's men. The general evidence is that both sides treated such men as routine prisoners of war, even where their origins were of a Special Forces nature. The following three cases date from this period.

a. **First Levitha Party: October 1943**

On 17 October 1943 the schooner HMS Hedgehog of the Levant Schooner Flotilla departed from the island of Stampalia carrying approximately forty German prisoners of war who had been captured on the island. She was forced to put into Levitha with engine trouble. By the night of the 18th the German prisoners appear to have overcome their British captors, whom they outnumbered by about five to one. They then dealt with the small garrison of about ten Italians and used the radio there to summon aid from the German garrison on the island of Cos (1).

The news of the German prisoners' successful escape and the capture of the British force seems to have been first received by the Luftwaffe (German Air Force) and they notified Headquarters Army Group E. Lt. Waldheim, who had been given this information, passed it to the Chief of Staff at 1640 hours on 19 October 1943 and was told ten minutes later to order the Luftwaffe to organise the pick up by aircraft of the British prisoners and the simultaneous deliveries of weapons and other necessaries to the German force now in control of the island:

> Major-General Winter gave Lt. Waldheim an order to be passed on to the Airforce that Army Group E wished the prisoners should be collected from Levitha by Junker [transport aircraft] and German weapons and other necessary items carried out there. (Annex 149).

In the subsequent discussions within Headquarters Army Group E on the situation on Levitha and future plans, Waldheim played no part and the matter was handled through the operations—Ia—channels. The incident was recorded in the Ic/AO Evening report for 19 October 1943 (Annex 150).

British records show seven British personnel (one naval officer, five naval ORs and one army OR) to have been captured. As most schooners had a small Greek crew, this may well account for the discrepancy between these seven men and the Germans' claims of eleven prisoners. Unfortunately British records do not contain details of any Greek personnel in this case.

On 21 October 1943 the Red Cross authorities in Athens recorded the presence of the naval officer as a prisoner of war in German hands in the transit camp in Athens (Annex 151). All seven men were moved to prisoner of war camps in Germany and survived the war. Their post-liberation reports make no reference to any illegal treatment while in the area under Army Group E's control. Only one man (the army OR) mentions being interrogated in Greece, recording: 'Athens 4.10.1943 ordinary interrogation' (2). The naval personnel were all routinely interrogated in prisoner of war camps in Germany.

There is no evidence that any of the men were taken to Salonika for interrogation, or treated as anything other than ordinary prisoners of war.

b. **Second Levitha Party: Lt. Sutherland, Black Watch and Lt. Kay, Border Regt.**

Following the capture by the Germans of the island of Levitha, it was decided that it was vital that the enemy garrison should be liquidated. The LRDG was given this task which they undertook on the night 23/24 October 1943. A force of some fifty was involved, divided into two groups commanded by Lts. Sutherland and Kay respectively, with Capt. Olivey in overall command.

The attack against the well-prepared Germans failed after hard fighting and only Capt. Olivey and seven others escaped to rendezvous with the boats the next night. A further visit by the boats failed to contact any more of the men.

German records noted that some thirty British prisoners were believed to have been involved in the operation, revising downwards their initial and in fact more correct estimate that forty to forty five men had been involved (Annexes 152 and 153). There are no references to 'commandos' in describing any of these men or their operations in the German documents.

The post-capture experiences of two of the LRDG other ranks are given in a book on the LRDG*. This records that on 26 October the two officers (Lt. Sutherland and Lt. Kay) and the wounded were evacuated to Piraeus harbour in Greece by flying boat: the remainder of the party followed later. On 2 November the party marched through Athens where they entrained in wagons for Germany. On 4 November the train passed through Salonika and on 5 November crossed the border into Yugoslavia. Soon after the two other ranks escaped with two other members of the force. The remainder of the prisoners ended up in standard prisoner of war camps in Germany.

The onward passage of Lt. Kay and Lt. Sutherland to the prisoner of war camp at Lückenwalde is noted in the Army Group E papers (Annex 154), a fact confirmed by Lt. Kay's post-liberation debrief (Annex 155). There is no evidence that any of these men of the LRDG, captured during this large scale fighting in the Aegean and Dodecanese islands, were treated other than as ordinary prisoners of war, and they were passed through to standard prisoner of war camps.

c. **Leros Party: F/Lt. Ogilvie, RAF**

F/Lt. Ogilvie was serving as a staff officer responsible for Air Support and Liaison with the Raiding Forces in the Aegean and was based on the island of Leros, where he was captured on 17 November 1943 after the Allied forces there surrendered to the German invasion force.

His recent testimony (3) is that the German Commander on the island showed him a copy of the 'infamous Commando Order dated 18.10.42' but assured him that he would not allow Ogilvie to be affected by its provisions. Ogilvie was moved by boat to Piraeus with a large number of other British servicemen, Greeks and Italians (all captured on Leros). Some of these men, including Ogilvie, were able to escape and make their way into Athens in a group, hoping to contact the partisans. However this party were arrested by the German military police and taken to a barracks where Ogilvie and another British officer were interrogated. This 'was conducted brutally' at what he believed to be the SD Headquarters in Athens. His incarceration there continued until 20 November 1943 when he was moved to a transit camp on the outskirts of Athens, apparently on the orders of higher authority who, he believed, had taken steps to register the men's presence with the Red Cross.

From the transit camp he and a number of other prisoners of war were taken to a military airfield where they were met by the escorting officer. He states that the officer introduced himself as 'Waldheim' and said that he was their escorting officer to Salonika en route to Germany. The officer was accompanied only by an SS soldier.

* D. Lloyd Owen, Providence Their Guide, Harrap, London. 1980.

Ogilvie says that, during the flight from Athens to Salonika, Lt. Waldheim asked for the prisoners' Identity Discs which were then replaced by some from legitimate corpses (i.e. from troops who had served in units that could not be considered to be 'commandos'). This might have helped disguise the prisoners' identities if they had previously been considered to be 'commandos'.

On arrival at the airfield at Salonika the party were kept in a hangar for some seven days during which period all six or seven Allied prisoners were driven out to the German Headquarters outside Salonika. There F/Lt. Ogilvie was interrogated by a German Air Force officer but also saw and spoke to the officer who called himself Waldheim. On the second visit, just before the group's departure, they were kept overnight in the Headquarters villa before being driven to the railhead where they joined a train of prisoners of war bound for Germany. Ogilvie states that, on arrival at the Air Force prisoner of war transit camp in Germany, he was more fully interrogated.

F/Lt. Ogilvie has said recently that, when he was liberated and repatriated to the United Kingdom in March 1945, he told his debriefers about these events but was told to forget all about them and that his official debrief form did not therefore include any reference to these events.

It is correct that both the first official debrief completed by him, which he has recently seen, and the other contemporary, then 'Top Secret' debrief, as well as his casualty questionnaire, make no mention whatsoever of any of the events detailed above as having occurred following his capture on Leros (Annexes 156–158).

The contemporary Red Cross records from Greece list F/Lt. Ogilvie under his own rather than under another's name. They show him as being among fifty-eight prisoners of war en route from Athens to Salonika (Annex 159). A later list from Salonika includes him among thirty-two prisoners of war known to be in Salonika and for whom 'capture cards' were available (Annex 160). Further reports from the Red Cross to the United Kingdom advising of his presence as a prisoner of war in Greece all use his own name.

Other evidence shows that the Germans regarded these men captured at this time on Leros and the other islands as ordinary prisoners of war. Although there were 'commandos' among the troops on the islands in the shape of men from the LRDG as well as SAS and SBS, the German view seems to have been that the garrison was a proper military force engaged in recognisable, formal military operations and as such its men would automatically be regarded as prisoners of war: they had not been operating behind German lines or on a hit-and-run raid (Annex 161).

The 'Commando Order' was a highly classified document on a very limited distribution and unlikely to be on hand to a lower level field commander engaged in active operations. Copies had been largely withdrawn in 1942/3 even from higher headquarters so that even the Ic of Army Group E's Headquarters himself had to approach the OKW for a copy some months later.

On the question of the custody of prisoners of war in Salonika, the documentary evidence and the personal testimony from both German and British sources indicates that prisoners were kept either in the transit camp for prisoners of war in the town of Salonika or, if of especial interest to the Germans, in one of the GFP prisons (also in the town) where interrogations could take place in suitably secure and isolated conditions (4).

F/Lt. Ogilvie's current recollections of events are therefore difficult to reconcile with the considerable body of evidence on the subject of the Germans' views and actions in these matters and such contemporary documentary evidence as survives on his own case.

d. **First Force 133 Party, Greece: Sgt. McCullough, Northamptonshire Regt. and a German deserter**

Sgt. McCullough (who was a member of the AMM) and a German deserter (who was assisting the AMM) were captured by the Germans on 6 February 1944 following a German anti-partisan sweep through the mountains which overran an AMM air-supply dropping ground.

The details of their subsequent treatment are very sparse. They were held for a period in what McCullough called the 'Gestapo' prison in Athens before being sent in March 1944 to Stalag VIIA at Mooseburg in Germany where further interrogation was carried out by specialist interrogators. Both soldiers then passed to other prisoner of war camps.

Sgt. McCullough remained in captivity until May 1945 when he was repatriated to the United Kingdom. The German escaped from a prisoner of war camp in May 1944. There is no report by McCullough of any ill-treatment after his capture (Annex 162).

e. **Second Force 133 Party, Greece: Capt. R. McGregor, RA and C. Capsis (Greek interpreter holding an honorary British commission)**

On 12 April, Capt. McGregor (a member of Force 133 serving with the AMM) entered a village with his interpreter C. Capsis, disregarding the villagers' warnings that there were Germans in the area. The two men were captured by the Germans, this being recorded in Army Group E's evening report for that day (Annex 163). Although they were clearly members of the AMM and involved in some way with the partisans, both men were reported to the Red Cross.

In the case of Capsis his presence in the Averoff prison in Athens was noted by the Red Cross on 25 April 1944 and their record shows that he had declared his service with the AMM (Annex 164). The authorities in London received initial details of his capture from the Swiss in Athens on 13 June 1944 (Annex 165).

Capt. McGregor was seen in the Averoff prison in Athens on about the 8 July 1944 by another British serviceman who recorded McGregor's move to Germany at about the end of July. This fits with the details in Red Cross records which on 10 August 1944 show that he had been in the Averoff prison until 31 July 1944 when he was transferred to the Transit Camp in Athens (Dulag 135) (Annex 166). The British authorities were advised by the Swiss at the end of August that both Capsis and McGregor were in the Averoff prison charged with acts of sabotage on account of their collaboration with Greek partisans (Annex 167). McGregor was in fact flown to Germany to the Mooseburg camp. There, on 10 August, he met Capsis again. Both men survived the war and were repatriated. British records relating to them make no mention of illegal treatment whilst in German hands (5).

Credit for the survival of these two men was claimed by a wartime German officer, Col. Kleykamp, who said he reported the two men's presence to the Red Cross hoping thereby to frustrate the requirements of the 'Commando Order'. Gen. Felmy (Kleykamp's commanding officer) apparently gave strong personal support to Kleykamp's action. After the war, both McGregor and Capsis agreed to Kleykamp's request and provided an affidavit describing their treatment for use in Felmy's defence during his war crimes trial (Annex 168).

f. **Force 133 Individual, Greece: Cpl. J. H. O'Neill, R Sigs.**

A member of the AMM operating in civilian clothes, Cpl. O'Neill was captured outside a Greek village on 1 July 1944 and was taken to the nearest German Headquarters and questioned rather violently. The Germans, it seems, were interested more in political questions than military information. However, his cover story—that he was an escaped prisoner of war from among the large number of men captured on the island of Leros—was apparently accepted and after a week he was sent to the Averoff prison, called by him the 'Gestapo' prison. After further interrogations and a stay of two months, during which he met Capt. McGregor who was also a prisoner there, he was sent on about 3 September 1944 as an ordinary prisoner of war first to the transit camp (Dulag 135) in Athens and then on about 1 October 1944 to the Transit Camp in Salonika (Dulag 185) (6). His existence and location were now admitted by the Germans to the Red Cross whose records in Athens note his presence in Dulag 135 on 4 September and his onward movement bound for Germany between 22–25 September via Salonika, where the Salonika Red Cross noted his presence on 6 October (Annex 169).

Force 133, with help from MI9/A Force, were also following his progress and attempting to free him and other prisoners but could not achieve this before the men's departure for Germany. Cpl. O'Neill was in a group of prisoners including Sgt. Dryden and two members of the Greek Sacred Squadron. O'Neill and the last two managed to escape from the train in Yugoslavia and make contact with the partisans. O'Neill's records provide few details of his imprisonment but make no mention of illegal treatment apart from his initial handling on capture (7).

g. **RSR/Force 133 Party, Greece: Sgt. R. C. Jones, MM, R. Sigs; Cpl. D. Lumb, RAMC; L/Cpl. S. Hayhurst, LIR; Pte. R. V. Wayman, Essex Regt; Pte. P. E. Daines; Essex Regt.**

Sgt. Jones, who had been in Greece since March 1943 with the AMM as a radio operator, was part of a mixed AMM and RSR party operating in Macedonia in July 1944 when the Germans launched a major drive through the area (probably 'Operation Steinadler').The other four men were from the RSR party. On 8 or 12 July 1944 (sources differ) the British force was making a night march to avoid the Germans. At first light there was a shouted warning 'Germans' and the party scattered in order to hide: in fact the newcomers were not Germans but another

Allied party. When the force re-assembled, Sgt. Jones and the four RSR men were missing and remained so in spite of various search parties being sent out to look for them. Later, after the German drive was over, a Greek interpreter (who had been with the party and had run in the same direction as the missing men) re-established contact with the main British force and reported that he and the five Britons had been hiding in a wood when a German patrol had entered and captured the others: the Greek being in a different position had not been noticed (8). Their capture was notified to the RSR headquarters in Italy later that month (Annex 170).

There are a few surviving references to this group of men in German records. On 17 July 1944 the Ic/AO Branch of Army Group E reported to Ic/AO Army Group F the results of the preliminary short interrogation of the five prisoners. This identified the Sergeant (evidently Jones) as someone who had parachuted into Greece some sixteen months before. The other four soldiers were identified as belonging to the convoy intercepted at Yannina on 6 May 1944 (Annex 171).

The E Ic/AO report for 1 August 1944 contained a brief comment (based on information from interrogation of prisoners) which dealt with the strength of the Allied Special Forces in the area (Annex 172). The details are broadly similar to the information apparently gleaned by the Germans from the interrogation of Sgt. Jones. This last is included in a file on source material on the organisation of the partisans. This interrogation discusses the role of the AMM personnel in relation to what it terms 'sabotage acts'. The report says that, according to Jones, apart from the liaison officers, there was a substantial group of Engineer officers who, supported by several British NCOs, organised demolitions and similar 'sabotage acts'. He apparently stressed that the responsibility for demolitions—'sabotage' to the Germans—lay with the AMM personnel and not with the RSR who were ordinary 'fighting troops'. It is possible that Jones was trying to protect the RSR individuals captured with him by disassociating them from 'sabotage' actions (Annex 173). A further brief reference to information from two British servicemen captured during the same German operation suggests from its content that these individuals were probably from the RSR and therefore from Sgt. Jones' party as no other RSR men appear to have been captured at that time (Annex 174).

The contemporary Red Cross records dated 31 July 1944 show that the whole party was taken to Salonika and put in the GFP prison. The Red Cross noted that it was not clear whether the Germans would treat them as prisoners of war or would consider them to be 'partisans' (Annex 175), with the implication of less favourable treatment.

Of the five men, all of whom survived the war, a post-liberation debrief written in 1945 survives only for Cpl. Lumb (Annex 176). It records that he was interrogated in Salonika on 18 July 1944, and that he was held in solitary confinement for nineteen days and was kept in handcuffs for five days. He recorded that he was sent to a prisoner of war camp, arriving at Mooseburg (Stalag VIIA) on 6 September 1944. In the case of Sgt. Jones, in spite of his being clearly identified with 'sabotage' carried out by the AMM, there is no record of any illegal treatment by the Germans (9).

h. **SBS Party, Crete: Lt. Lodwick, General List and Bdr. Nixon, RA**

In July 1944 Lt. Lodwick was in command of D Patrol of L Detachment SBS which, in conjunction with others, had been tasked with the destruction of German stocks of petrol on the island of Crete. His party was on the island for some three weeks reconnoitering the target area.

On the night of 22 July 1944 an attack was launched on a petrol dump at the western end of the island. The patrol was split into two parties in order to lay charges on both sides of the targeted dump. When one of these parties became involved in a fight with a number of German sentries, the resulting German activity prevented the other party (Lodwick and his sole companion Bdr. Nixon) from making contact with either the other party or the Greek guides. Lodwick, therefore, set off for a more distant pre-arranged rendezvous and he and Nixon had succeeded in evading the Germans for well over an hour until the close proximity of large numbers of Germans, some with guard dogs, and the fact that the terrain was now well-lit by the glare from the exploding petrol dump, forced the pair to take cover in a nearby ditch. Although they remained undetected for about another four hours, eventually a police dog scented them. After some 45 minutes of barking had attracted the Germans' attention sufficiently for them to begin to search the ditch itself, the British pair were forced to surrender. The German reports of the action mention both their capture and the general events of the raid, seen as sabotage (Annex 177).

Both men were taken to the GFP Headquarters in Crete where Lt. Lodwick was interrogated at length by a number of officers. Lodwick was aware of the need to conceal the fact that members of his party were to remain on the island for three more days. He also considered that, in view of the somewhat precarious position of the German garrison on the island which had been explained to him by officers from Force 133 during the preceding three weeks, he might be able to secure the capitulation of the garrison. From the outset he demanded to see the island's Commander (Gen. Müller), maintaining that the destruction of the petrol dumps had merely been a demonstration of the Germans' hopeless position and the urgent need for negotiations to avoid pointless bloodshed. Although he did not see Gen. Müller, he did see four of his staff officers and believed that only the opposition of the GFP prevented his achieving the desired interview (Annexes 178 and 179).

The Germans, certainly those on the island commander's staff, took Lt. Lodwick's story seriously and discussions were held with him on the ways and means by which the negotiations would be organised. Lodwick said that he would remain as a hostage while Bdr. Nixon escorted a German officer to Cairo. Fortunately Lodwick was able to communicate with Nixon by passing notes through a friendly Polish-German guard in the prison so that he was able to back up Lodwick's story.

However, the GFP, in whose prison they were still held, claimed that as members of a 'commando' unit they could not be regarded as prisoners of war and would be shot. These threats were repeated especially to Nixon: indeed, the GFP were most insistent that the men could not possibly be regarded as prisoners of war because of previous 'commando outrages'. They waged a form of psychological warfare by coming to the cell at night with an armed guard, rattling the door and leading Lodwick out—just to give him a drink of water. The two men were still in solitary confinement without exercise outside their cells and given for the most part only poor rations. Their existence as prisoners in German hands was known by the British as a result of local intelligence and efforts were made by the various British Force 133 and A Force officers on the island to free them but these came to nought.

The threatened executions did not materialize. Unbeknown to the prisoners their story had been taken quite seriously at Army Group level and on 17 August 1944 Lt. Col. Warnstorff (the Ic at E's Headquarters) had approached his superior (Lt. Col. von Harling) in Army Group F, as he believed that the proposed visit of a German to Cairo would be a useful intelligence mission in its own right: Warnstorff even suggested the name of a suitable officer to act as the German emissary (Annex 180). This suggestion was passed by F to the appropriate political foreign affairs department on 19 August (Annex 181) and on 23 August the two Britons were moved by sea from Crete to Athens where they arrived on 26th. They were placed in the Averoff prison, again largely in solitary confinement, and subjected to further interrogation by (among others) a Colonel from Army Group E. Nixon was especially subjected to threats of execution. While in Athens they were permitted to exercise in the prison yard and met other British servicemen also imprisoned there, including Sgt. Dryden from the Calino party.

On 31 August 1944 the two Britons were flown to Salonika, apparently on the orders of the Army Group E Headquarters, and were put in the GFP prison. They were again questioned on their story: according to Lt. Lodwick's post-war comments, it was all but accepted as fact and arrangements were put in hand for the passage of Nixon and a German officer to the Allied controlled areas. At this point, however, the defection of Germany's ally Bulgaria on 9 September 1944 ended all negotiations. The two men remained in the GFP prison and were joined there by several other Allied prisoners (two from the RSR, 'Cpl. Brookes and Pte. Chewerton' (see Section i), and three Greeks from the Greek Sacred Squadron captured on a naval vessel off one of the Aegean islands (see Section j)). Lodwick and Nixon's existence was now known to the Red Cross in Athens who on 16 September formally recorded their detention in the Averoff prison from 26 to 31 August 1944 (Annex 182).

The British were also now aware of their latest movements, A Force/MI9 having tracked them to Athens and then on to Salonika. Lodwick and Nixon were among the group of prisoners mentioned in radio messages between various Allied agencies, one of which (on 10 October 1944, according to the contemporary diary of a British warrant officer serving with the Allied Military Liaison team) mentioned 'six British other ranks held at a house in Salonika awaiting early execution' (10). British efforts to free them, however, could not reach fruition before their departure from the 'Konigan Olga Street' prison on 7 or 8 October. However two men then managed to escape leaving only four Britons, escorted by 'GFP and S.S', to be placed on a train for Germany. Force 133 were then able to report on 20 October 1944:

British have not been shot. They left for Germany on 8th October. A certain Capt. Ludovic [i.e. Lodwick] was in command of the group. The names of the other five could not be taken (11).

The train had to halt at Mitrovica in Serbia (Yugoslavia) because the railway had been cut further north by Allied action. The party were taken to the local prisoner of war camp where they also met Capt. G. Barkham (a Force 133 Officer captured in Crete in civilian clothes (see Section 1)). In his book on his wartime career, Lt. Lodwick describes how the young German Intelligence Colonel from the Salonika Headquarters visited them on 1 November 1944 to tell them of the liberation of Salonika by the SBS. This is believed to be Lt. Col. Warnstorff, the Ic in Army Group E, whose Headquarters had withdrawn northwards to Mitrovica in mid October.

On 5 November 1944 the British party, as well as a number of captured American airmen, Russians and Bulgarians, were marched northwards under guard only to be freed when the partisans surrounded the party on 7 November 1944.

The treatment of the party whilst in prison, especially on Crete, demonstrates the Germans' view, or at least that of the GFP, of the status of 'commandos'—even at this late stage of the war. The prisoners were certainly not treated by them wholly in accordance with the requirements of the Geneva Convention covering prisoners of war. Clearly the existence of the two prisoners was known to Army Group E and the evidence suggests that the officer who visited them in Athens was Lt. Col. Warnstorff (the Ic). The conditions in which they were then being kept will almost certainly have been known to him. On the other hand, there is no evidence of deliberate physical maltreatment and the men were, albeit belatedly, treated as prisoners of war.

i. **RSR Party, Greece: Cpl. R. J. Brookes, RAMC and Pte. T. A. J. Chiverton, Sussex Regt.**

Army Group E's Ic/AO 'Evening Situation Report' for 22 August 1944 (Annex 183) contains an entry that two British soldiers had been captured by a unit in the Lamia area. British records indicate that two RSR men (Cpl. R. J. Brookes and Pte. T. A. J. Chiverton) were captured about this time (Annex 184). Following their capture, unsuccessful efforts were made to liberate them with the help of A Force (Annex 185). As has already been seen, these two men joined Lt. Lodwick and Bdr. Nixon in the prison in Salonika on about 31 August 1944 and formed part of their party which was eventually liberated by the partisans near Sarajevo. Unfortunately their own records are very sparse and provide few specific details but they make no mention of any illegal treatment having occurred.

j. **'Commando'/Naval Party, Sirina**

As part of the Raiding Forces activity, a reconnaissance patrol from the Greek Sacred Squadron was despatched to the Aegean island of Scarpanto towards the end of August 1944, on board vessels from the Royal Navy of which one was Motor Launch (ML) 1381. After landing, the patrol entered a minefield and received a number of casualties. The crews of the vessels heard the explosions and returned to the island to evacuate the patrol, which they achieved without hindrance from the Germans. ML 1381 then sailed to Sirina, the nearest unoccupied island, to lie up until the next night.

Unfortunately, the Germans had identified the activities of the Raiding Forces in establishing observation posts on the various islands and reporting on German ship and air traffic. Accordingly, on 23 August 1944, they had set in motion 'Operation Wanderfalke' designed to locate and eliminate such posts. The forces deployed came from the Brandenbergers' Coastal Patrol Company using two small Assault Boats and a number of larger landing craft (I Boats) in support, usually one of the latter to each pair of Assault Boats. They carried out a systematic sweep of the area, visiting the islands.

According to a contemporary German report, on the morning of the 26 August 1944, two Assault Boats and an I Boat approached the northern coast of Sirina and came under machine gun fire. During a pause in the fire, the I Boat and one of the Assault Boats managed to land their men on the east side of the bay. The other Assault Boat crossed to the west side of the bay and was again engaged by machine gun fire but suffered no casualties and landed its men. The eastern German party reached the vicinity of the British boat first and, after a brief close quarter battle, the British force surrendered. It consisted of two officers and eleven other ranks as well as five Greeks from the Greek Sacred Squadron.

The German operational commander ordered all other I Boats to go to the area and in due course the captured British vessel and its crew were brought to Stampalia, reaching the island at about 1600 hours. The prisoners were transferred to the custody of the island's garrison (12).

The successful action was reported to the German Commander East Aegean on the evening of 26 August. This report stated that three of the eighteen prisoners were wounded and that, although some signals information had been recovered, all the secret papers had been destroyed before capture (Annex 186).

In the afternoon of 27 August 1944, the German forces on Stampalia advised the Commander on Rhodes that the party did not form part of a 'commando' operation (Annex 187), although in fact it was no less of a 'commando' raid than that of the Alimnia party.

On the British side, by the evening of 28 August 1944 the Raiding Force HQ had reported the fact that ML1381 had failed to rendezvous with another British vessel. On the same day another vessel visited Sirina and was told of ML1381's capture (Annex 188). The details of the crew were passed to the Admiralty on 30 August: the next day the next of kin were advised that the men were 'missing'.

In the meantime on 29 August 1944, the Germans had transferred the prisoners to the island of Leros where the officers and two of the senior other ranks were formally interrogated and the captured intelligence material was handed over to the island's Ic. According to the post-war liberation reports of these men, their interrogations were perfectly proper and there were no threats or violence (Annex 189).

In due course the prisoners were moved to the Greek mainland to the prisoner of war transit camp at Athens and from there to prisoner of war camps in Germany which they all reached on or soon after 2 October 1944. In some cases they had communicated with their next of kin through the Red Cross within a few days of arrival in Germany. All the British members of the party survived the war.

The information on the Greek personnel is less complete but it is known from Capt. Lodwick's report that three Greeks, including Capt. Costelatos (the leader of the patrol) joined him for a short while in the GFP prison in Salonika. Capt. Costelatos is also among three Greeks from the Sacred Squadron recorded on 27 September 1944 by the Red Cross as being in Salonika (Annex 190). Two of them, including Capt. Costelatos, escaped with another British serviceman while en route to a camp in Germany.

k. **RSR Individual, Greece: Lt. I. Williams, RA**

Lt. Williams was a member of the RSR operating in Greece whose party clashed with a German patrol in the Kozani area on 10 or 11 September 1944. In the ensuing fighting Lt. Williams was captured (Annex 191). His capture is reported in the Army Group E Ic 'Evening Report' for 11 September (Annex 192). There is no further mention of him in surviving German documents. The Red Cross in Salonika recorded his presence as a prisoner on 28 September (Annex 193). British records provide no details of his captivity save to show that he was a prisoner in Greece between 11 September and 23 October 1944 and then in Yugoslavia from 23 October to 28 December 1944. After this date he was moved to a camp in Germany from which he was liberated in 1945.

l. **Force 133 Individual, Crete: Capt. G. G. A. Barkham, Beds & Herts Regt.**

Capt. Barkham (a member of Force 133) was captured by the Germans on the island of Crete on 16 October 1944. At the time of his capture he was apparently not in uniform but was wearing civilian clothes: this placed him in serious danger of being treated as a spy and not as a prisoner of war. Apparently he employed a cover story similar to that used by Lt. Lodwick several months earlier, i.e. that he was in effect an emissary to offer terms to the German garrison commander.

On 19 October 1944, he was flown to Salonika and then moved north to Mitrovica, the journey by train taking a week because of air and partisan attacks. At Mitrovica Capt. Barkham was interrogated by what he called the HQ Intelligence Branch. Recent testimony from Cpl. Wollschläger described his interrogation at Mitrovica of a British officer who had been captured on Crete (13). This would seem to be Capt. Barkham. He was apparently told that his being in civilian clothes put his captors in an awkward position as they wished to be fair. Sticking to his cover story Barkham was then briefly interrogated by a Lt. Colonel about thirty years old who was introduced to him as the head of the Intelligence Branch. The Lt. Colonel was very courteous and, after a short conversation with another German officer, asked Barkham why he was in civilian clothing. He seemed to accept Barkham's account and said that he need not worry further, at least for the moment, as he would send him to the prisoner of war camp in Mitrovica. He took him to the German officers' mess and gave him some excellent cognac before the other officer escorted him to the prison camp where he met Lt. Lodwick and his companions. In due course Capt. Barkham was liberated by the partisans together with Lodwick and the other men.

Barkham summarised his treatment by the Germans as very good, considering that he could not rightly claim to be a prisoner of war. At no time did they use any form of physical torture in their interrogations though they did tell him that he would probably be shot. The conditions at Mitrovica were very bad but the camp staff were apparently friendly and decent to the prisoners (Annex 194).

m. **Individual Evader Crete/Greece: Pte. Turton, Yorks & Lancs Regt.**

This soldier had evaded capture after the fall of Crete to the Germans in 1941. He had eventually been forced to surrender to the Germans in 1944 following an injury for which he required medical treatment. He was subsequently held in the Averoff Prison and later in the cells of what his fellow prisoners called the 'Gestapo' headquarters in Athens where he was seen by Sgt. J. Dryden (cf. p. 77) and with whom he shared a cell for six days, after which Dryden was moved away.

Following the Allied liberation of Athens, British war crimes investigators found evidence of Pte. Turton's imprisonment and located some surviving Greeks who had been imprisoned with him as well as obtaining information from Sgt. Dryden (see Annex 147). These investigations revealed that on the morning of 28 September 1944 shortly before the Germans evacuated Athens Turton had been taken from the so called 'Gestapo' headquarters with several Greeks and in all probability shot, this being the contemporary comment of a German guard at the prison to a Greek prisoner who survived the war.

Although the investigations established the identities of a number of SS and SD men who were believed to be implicated in this deed, none fell into Allied hands, and the case was left untried (Annex 195).

There is no evidence in contemporary documents that Army Group E Headquarters was involved in Pte. Turton's treatment and fate.

n. **The Laterina Case**

This case concerns the illegal shooting of Allied prisoners of war from the camp at Laterina in Italy. Allegations have been made fairly recently that Lt. Waldheim was linked with this incident.

The allegations came from a former British serviceman (Mr Frank Notley) who said that he was an eyewitness to the return to the prisoner of war camp at Laterina in Italy in late September 1943 of the bodies of some thirty Allied prisoners of war who had been killed by the Germans during the move of a party of prisoners from the camp the day before. Mr Notley has said that Lt. Waldheim arrived at the camp by car soon after the bodies were returned there and that he seemed to be in charge of the situation, as all around 'paid respects' to him. It has been inferred, therefore, that Lt. Waldheim was in some way responsible for the shooting (14).

A detailed examination of the history of the prisoner of war camp at Laterina shows that the only incident that bears any resemblance to these events took place in mid June 1944 when a column of some 2500 British, American and other Allied prisoners of war were marched from Laterina Camp some 18 kilometers towards the nearest railway station at Monte Vachi. During the march there were a number of attempts to escape from the column: some prisoners of war dropped into ditches beside the road and hid, more ran into the fields alongside the road or hid in the nearby bushes, and others tried to hide in a village which the column passed through in the dark. Some of these last hid in an alley, others took refuge in a bedroom in a house. Other prisoners fell out of the column with permission to relieve themselves.

These escape attempts were generally answered by the guards with gunfire, even when prisoners of war stopped and made to re-surrender themselves or made no further effort to get away. Several men were shot repeatedly when already wounded and even men who had fallen out with permission were shot. The men in the bedroom were all killed when a hand-grenade was thrown through the window, as was an Italian girl also in the room. The exact number of dead is unclear but many sworn eye-witness accounts, from men in the column itself, suggest that some fourteen or fifteen men were killed. The next morning, having spent the remainder of the night in a field, the column returned to Laterina on foot as no train was available. After the prisoners of war had reached Laterina camp, having seen some of the dead prisoners of war's bodies still lying along the route, a truck came to the camp with twelve bodies, one of them that of the Italian girl. There are eye-witness accounts of the arrival of the truck and the number of bodies: it is clear however that not all the bodies of dead prisoners of war were there—some had been run over by heavy vehicles which passed along the column's route during the night and could not therefore be recovered (Annexes 196–198).

The unjustified shooting of surrendering escapers was registered by the British authorities as a war crime with the United Nations War Crimes Commission. The view of the British legal officers when preparing the case was that responsibility for the shootings rested primarily with the guards, especially the guard commander Hoffman who was named by several witnesses as having shot a number of men himself. The Camp Commandant and his deputy or adjutant were held indirectly responsible because of their duty to maintain discipline among their subordinates. Although it was accepted that some of the shootings might have been justifiable, at least ten were not.

Efforts were made by British and American authorities to trace the perpetrators (Annex 199). Some nine of the camp personnel including the camp officer were identified: Lt. Waldheim's name was not among them. Neither Hoffman nor any of the others appear to have been traced.

There is nothing to corroborate the recently suggested presence of Lt. Waldheim in Italy at this time, or of any involvement by him with this affair. Following his liberation and repatriation from German captivity, Mr Notley completed a prisoner of war debrief form and also sent two detailed letters to the War Office in which he described his experiences both while in captivity and during his periods of liberty after his several escapes: he also included details of those who had helped him, to ensure that they received recognition. In none of these accounts did he mention any incident similar to that known to have taken place at Laterina. Indeed from his January 1946 account, it seems that, although he had been in the Laterina camp both in 1943 and again briefly in 1944 (leaving early in June of that year) Mr Notley was already in Mantua (well to the north) at the time of the incident. Subsequently he was held in Mooseburg, from where early reports of the incident were made, that being also the destination of other prisoners from Laterina (Annex 200).

Overview of the cases examined

These cases cover all the British Special Forces personnel captured in the relevant area and period whom it has been possible to identify and who represent almost, if not all, such personnel. Examination of these cases has made it possible to take an overview of them and of German attitudes with some confidence.

The pattern that emerges is of an initial classification of prisoners by the Germans. Those considered as 'commandos' were usually withheld from the normal prisoner of war administrative process and held by the counter-intelligence and security police organisation at least until their interrogation was complete.

After capture, many if not all were threatened with execution as 'saboteurs', 'terrorists' etc. But, of the total of thirty, only seven did not survive the war and are believed to have been executed by the Germans.

It is difficult to determine the precise reasons for this outcome which, given the interest of Lt. Col. von Harling (the Ic of Army Group F) in the application of the 'Commando Order' on a wide scale, seems somewhat strange. In the earlier discussion of the German attitude to the 'Commando Order', the confusion in its application was demonstrated and the record of cases shows a less than strict observance of its requirements. However, there is little hard evidence to support any claim that this confusion was a key factor.

There may also be some truth in the claims of the German staff officers from the area that they sought to evade the 'Commando Order' whenever possible: there is of course some contemporary evidence to support this, most notably Capt. Barkham's experiences at Army Group E's headquarters in late October 1944. Further, in the contemporary British documents the actions of the Red Cross, the Swiss and Swedish Consuls are also credited (and deservedly so) with an important contribution to ensuring captives' treatment as ordinary prisoners of war, although it must be noted that being recorded by the Red Cross as a prisoner of war did not exclude being subject later to Sonderbehandlung (as some other cases have shown).

In the final analysis there is no concrete evidence to account for the execution of just these seven men who were captured in two separate incidents in March and April 1944. However, during the trial of various senior German Army officers before an American Military Tribunal at Nuremberg in 1947, one of the witnesses stated that the British 'commando' raids on two Greek islands in February 1944 had not only been noted by the OKW (cf. p. 30) but also that Hitler himself had been aware of the incidents and had been angered by them: as a result, a signal was sent by the OKW to Army Group F in which 'renewed reference' was made to the 'Commando Order' (Annex 201). It is possible, therefore, that since the Alimnia prisoners were the first to be captured after these incidents and belonged to a party which was brought to the attention of the OKW and possibly Hitler, they became the unfortunate victims of Hitler's and the OKW's efforts to stop 'commando' raids by enforcing the 'Commando Order'. Any efforts or intentions of local German commanders to avoid such actions were frustrated by the involvement of Hitler in these matters. Capt. Warren's fate as a member of the Allied Military Mission is probably bound up with the insistence of Lt. Col. von Harling (the Ic of Army Group F) at the time in question that such individuals, as saboteurs, be treated as 'commandos' (cf. p. 30). It is clear that Capt. Warren had come to his attention and Warren's presumed date of execution also follows soon after the above mentioned reminder of the Order.

The execution of the Alimnia party and Capt. Warren, if they took place in 1944, would appear to have been the first identifiable treatment of Allied Special Forces personnel under the 'Commando Order' in Greece. A party of Force 133 men captured in Greece in April 1943, although earmarked in correspondence for such treatment (Annex 202), had in fact been passed to Germany and at least one man had been noted by the Red Cross en route (Annex 203). However, this party did not survive the war and are believed to have been executed in a Concentration Camp in April 1945.

One 'commando' (Sgt. Dryden), although earmarked for transfer to the SD, passed instead to a prisoner of war camp and survived the war. The involvement of Sgt. Jones of the AMM in 'sabotage' activities was clear from the report of his interrogation, yet he too survived.

The British Special Forces personnel captured later may have benefitted from a less high profile and perhaps from a reluctance by some German officers to take drastic action against such men once the success of the Allied landing in Normandy had reinforced the message that Germany had lost the war. Perhaps also, as outlined in Chapter 5, the on-going discussions in Berlin (which until August 1944 had reached no decision on the treatment to be given to captured AMM personnel) may have helped.

The cases of non-commando personnel in the Balkans examined here demonstrate that, with the exception of Pte. Turton, all received normal prisoner of war treatment and survived the war.

CHAPTER 10: References

(1) War Office files (PRO) WO 218: 91 and MOD Archives.

(2) MOD Archives.

(3) Correspondence with MOD and Thames Television.

(4) Thames Television and Austrian Commission, Correspondence with MOD.

(5) SOE Archives.

(6) SOE Archives.

(7) SOE Archives.

(8) SOE Archives.

(9) SOE Archives.

(10) Correspondence with G. Fleming Esq.

(11) SOE Archives.

(12) Bundesarchiv, Federal Republic of Germany.

(13) Correspondence with MOD.

(14) Correspondence with MOD.

Chapter 11: Summary of the evidence relating to Lt. Waldheim's involvement in the cases under review

Before considering this subject in detail, the overall position of the then Lt. Waldheim within the headquarters of Army Group E must be remembered. The examination of this aspect in Chapter 4 showed that there was no evidence of his having any 'command authority' of his own. (This term usually refers to the legal authority vested in an officer to give orders, normally of an operational nature, to field troops). There is no evidence of his having been personally involved in making command decisions, although he will often have been aware of many of the operational decisions made by his superiors.

Lt. Waldheim would clearly have been aware of the existence of any Allied Servicemen brought to Salonika for interrogation and he would have known that interrogations were taking place. Further, he may well have been involved in some of the discussions concerning areas or topics of particular interest to the Ic section and which should be covered during interrogations. He would certainly have later received any relevant information from these interrogations. He has however consistently and strongly denied any personal involvement in the actual interrogation of prisoners of war. This claim is supported both by the recent testimony of his colleagues in the Headquarters, several of whom have however said that they did carry out interrogations, and also by his predecessor (Lt. Schollen), who similarly denies having conducted any interrogations during his period of service in the headquarters at Arsakli (cf. p. 20).

Further, concerning the handling of prisoners brought to Salonika, there is no evidence that Lt. Waldheim had in any way a responsibility for the GFP or for its activities, or that he had any control over these. He has stated recently that he never visited a GFP prison (1). Responsibility lay with Lt. Col. Warnstorff, with the day to day control undertaken by the GFP's commander in conjunction with Maj. Hammer (the AO).

An examination of contemporary material, including that specifically relating to intelligence matters, has revealed no evidence to suggest that Lt. Waldheim was in any way a professional military intelligence officer or a member of a specialist German intelligence agency. No evidence has been found to support the statements by Cpl. J. Mayer that Lt. Waldheim was an 'espionage officer' and had close involvement with other counter-intelligence activities carried out by the SD (cf. p. 18).

The significance of signatures on documents

The signing of a document 'F.d.R.' (Für die Richtigkeit literally 'For the correctness') and also the initialling by individuals of the text of documents, are of significance: examples of both are to be found in contemporary documents relevant to this Review (Annex 204).

It was standard practice in the German Armed Forces of the period for documents of all kinds to be signed and initialled. The German Armed Forces Manual of 1939 on staff writing noted that Für die Richtigkeit was used to authenticate the correctness of the text of an abstract or copy (Annex 205). However, later in the war, according to the early post-war testimony of a senior German officer (Gen. Franz Halder, Chief of the Army General Staff from 1938–1942), Für die Richtigkeit was used to authenticate documents which, although issued by a senior officer and on his authority, were not signed personally by him. According to Halder, this later practice was not formally recorded in any of the manuals. Where the senior officer issuing the order had only prepared a draft, Für die Richtigkeit was used by a subordinate to authenticate the correctness of the neat text made from the draft. Further, where the item, especially with signals, was not signed but was concluded with the title block of the authorising section (e.g. 'OB Südost, Ic/AO Nr 1317g/Kdos'), Für die Richtigkeit signified that the text was a valid order in terms of the authority of the issuing section and that the contents reflected the decision of the authorising senior officer. Gen. Foertsch (the Chief of Staff of Army Group F in Belgrade between January 1943 and March 1944) also stated after the war that, in his headquarters, certain officers in the various headquarters' sections had to sign teleprinter messages despatched from the headquarters F.d.R. to confirm that the contents corresponded to the decision of the authorising or issuing officer. Both Generals agreed that signing F.d.R. did not carry any responsibility for the substance of the contents or indicate that the individual so signing was personally issuing the order on his own authority (Annexes 206 and 207).

The other abbreviation seen on documents 'F.d.R.A.'—(F.d.R. der Abschrift—literally 'for the correctness of the copy') means that the document was a true copy of an original which had been seen by the signatory, and seems to have been introduced in the war to distinguish between the earlier and later usage of F.d.R.

Initials on documents denoted both authorship and the author's certification that the transcript corresponded accurately to his original. Initials appeared usually at the end of the text but above the authorising signature block.

In some cases two separate officers initialled documents (e.g. Annexes 85 and 90). This would appear to be because one was testifying to the authorship of enclosures and the other to the text of the covering letter.

Summary of Lt. Waldheim's involvement in the major cases

The Cephalonia Case

The allegations in this case concerning the then Lt. Waldheim are that he was personally involved in the interrogation and general treatment of Capt. Warren; and that he prepared a report on Capt. Warren's interrogation in which he falsely described Capt. Warren as a saboteur thus bringing him within the terms of the 'Commando Order' so that he was subject to Sonderbehandlung and was executed.

From the date of the initial capture of the Cephalonia party until 16 April 1944 Lt. Waldheim was absent from the Headquarters of Army Group E on leave. Therefore he can have played no part in events prior to the latter date. By the time he returned the party had already been categorized by the local troops as a sabotage group; this designation had been repeated by higher headquarters right up to the OKW, and the question of Sonderbehandlung in accordance with the 'Commando Order' had already been raised by Army Group F.

The report of 8 May 1944 (cf. p. 42) from Army Group E is initialled with a 'W' at the end of the main text. An examination of other contemporary documentary evidence from the Headquarters of Army Group E indicates that this 'W' is the initial of Lt. Waldheim, and that he drafted the report. On the basis of the earlier discussions of the duties within the 03 subsection, there is no evidence that Lt. Waldheim himself would have conducted any of the interrogations. Indeed, given the range of languages spoken by this party, there were probably a number of separate interrogations conduced by several different interpreters. Lt. Waldheim's role was to collate and assess for intelligence purposes the information passed to him by his colleagues who had carried out and supervised the interrogations.

The use in the report of the word 'sabotage' has generated especial interest. The report in fact makes only one reference to sabotage and this in discussing the activities of the Greek partisans: without specifically describing Warren as a 'saboteur', this records his supposed comments on the reliability of the Greeks in carrying out demolitions:

> Warren believed the Greeks were too unreliable to be entrusted with sabotage operations on their own.

These comments could have been taken to imply that Warren himself did undertake sabotage, and this could explain why he was excluded when the remaining members of the party were taken out of the category of saboteurs.

The German view of such activities as demolitions by partisans or Allied troops such as 'commandos' as 'sabotage' has been covered earlier (cf. p. 34). While accepting that military demolitions should not necessarily be so defined, it is interesting to note in this connection contemporary Allied reports and directives on the subject of Allied Special Force operations in the theatre. These quite clearly list 'sabotage' as being among the tasks of such personnel (Annex 208 and 209). The post-war comments of some British participants agree. One recently recorded how the SOE officer who met him on his arrival in Greece gave him an unvarnished account of his experiences. These reflected his frustration 'as a trained saboteur' at the lack of damage he had been able to inflict on the Germans (2). Another account, produced just after the war, discussed the SOE's Greek operations and recorded how another SOE officer described his task there as 'sabotage' (3).

It seems therefore that not only was the use of the term 'sabotage' in this context not a deliberate distortion and represented the standard German view of such activities, but also that such terminology to describe these activities was not unique to the Germans.

The assessment of the strength of the supposed Allied network of agents in Greece and the possible Allied intentions to return the Russians to Greece later, by implication for work with the partisans or to suborn other Russians in German service, though incorrect, can be seen as a genuine assessment based on the Germans' view of the position and not as an attempt improperly to 'indict' the individuals.

From the previous examination of the attitude to the 'Commando Order' within the Balkan area under the command of Army Group F, it is clear that personnel of the Allied Military Mission were greatly at risk of being considered to fall within its provisions and of being treated accordingly, in spite of the attitude at that time of the OKW that such individuals should be accorded PW status. The infomation apparently given by Warren during his initial interrogation soon after capture that he had been dropped by parachute just as the voyage was beginning, would confirm his status as an AMM member in German eyes, apart from any later admission of his role as a liaison officer with the partisans as recorded in the report by Army Group E.

It may be concluded that the Report, compiled presumably by Lt. Waldheim and sent on the 8 May, was an expansion of information previously passed to and by higher formations while Lt. Waldheim was on leave, which had labelled the group as a 'Sabotagetruppe' and stated that Sonderbehandlung would be their fate. The subsequent interrogations may have correctly identified the Poles and Russians as deserters rather than 'commandos', but Capt. Warren's apparent statements made any alteration of his designation unlikely.

The Report thus represented a justifiable interpretation of the information gained from the previous interrogations, given the state of German knowledge and fears at the time. The words used to describe the activities of the party represented the normal German terminology of the time in referring to the work of partisans and their AMM helpers.

The Alimnia Party

It is alleged that, in the case of the Alimnia party of 'commandos', Lt. Waldheim played a criminally culpable part in the process of their handling and handover to the SD, thereby participating in the acts that led to their presumed unlawful killing.

The post-war British war crimes investigations into this case revealed no evidence against him. Subsequent research has shown that Lt. Waldheim was on leave in Austria from early March until 16 or 17 April 1944 and was therefore not present at Army Group E Headquarters during the time of the party's capture and the reporting of their existence up to the highest command (the OKW) and perhaps to Hitler himself. During this period a Wehrmachtbericht was also issued reporting the party as 'commandos' and indicating to the Germans by its wording that they would be treated as laid down by the 'Commando Order' and its ancillary letter.

After his return, Lt. Waldheim will have been aware of the men's existence as he will have seen the signals and letters concerning the subject that passed to and from the E Ic section including the intended transfer of the men to the SD (cf. p. 54).

He will also have been aware of their interrogation, but there is no evidence that he was involved in the fruitless interrogations in Salonika, either personally or by advising on treatment. Nor is there any evidence that he was responsible for liaison with the GFP or SD, these matters falling within the AO's responsibilities as did some responsibility for PW matters.

There is no evidence that Lt. Waldheim was the instigator, or even the sender, of the signal from E to F asking for instructions regarding the prisoners. His lack of any 'command authority' within the Branch to intervene in the matter and prevent their transfer to the SD has already been discussed (cf. p. 14).

There is no evidence, therefore, that his personal involvement was other than very limited or that he took a personal part in matters concerning the party's treatment and final disposal.

The Yannina Case

Current allegations are that Lt. Waldheim was involved in the interrogation, which included illegal treatment, of the British 'commandos' in the Yannina party and was responsible for the inadequate conditions in which they were imprisoned.

Contemporary work by United Kingdom war crimes investigators was based on the reports submitted by the four returned ex-prisoners of war in 1945-46. These, including Capt. Bluett's affidavit, provided details that led to the identification only of the GFP NCO 'Stoffberg'.

Current research shows that a report on the men's capture was sent to the Ic/AO Branch in Salonika and that the men themselves were sent to Salonika where they were imprisoned and interrogated. As Lt. Waldheim's job required him to be familiar with such reports and with the results of any interrogations (whether by subordinate formations, the GFP, or by the Army Group itself) he will clearly have been aware of these men's presence in Salonika. However there is no evidence to link Lt. Waldheim personally with the men's interrogation: the more recent statements by surviving 'commandos' provide no significant identification material. The responsibility for the conduct of such matters lay with Lt. Waldheim's colleagues who have testified to taking such decisions and to conducting an interrogation of Bluett and Hamilton, albeit without using any illegal measures (cf. p. 72).

Lt. Waldheim's lack of responsibility for the GFP, who ran the prison, has been identified. There is no evidence that Lt. Waldheim's personal involvement in this case was other than very limited.

The Calino Party

The current allegations against the then Lt. Waldheim in this case are that he was personally responsible for the interrogation and general treatment of these men whilst prisoners in German hands, and that he was involved in the decision (and perhaps personally gave the order) that Sgt. Dryden would be handed to the SD for Sonderbehandlung.

Of the individuals concerned with this case, only Pte. Doughty was brought to Salonika for interrogation by the staff of Army Group E. There is no evidence of any illegal actions during the interrogation which would seem to have been carried out by an NCO of the Ic section. Once it was established that Doughty was a medical orderly, he was properly treated as a prisoner of war and sent to a prisoner of war camp.

Sgt. Dryden, who remained in Athens until his transfer to a prisoner of war camp in Salonika en route to Germany, does not appear to have been interrogated by personnel of Army Group E. However the Army Group E report on the Calino raid, submitted to High Command South-East (Army Group F) on 18 July 1944 and initialled at the end of the second page with a 'W' believed to be Waldheim's, does state that Dryden was to be handed over to the SD in accordance with the 'Commando Order'.

This indicates that Lt. Waldheim was aware of Dryden's existence as a prisoner and he must have been aware of the implications of the proposal regarding Dryden's disposal. However there is no evidence that he initiated or authorised this statement or that he had any authority to alter it in any way.

The Laterina Case

There is no evidence that corroborates recent claims concerning the presence of Lt. Waldheim at Laterina. None of the sworn accounts of eye-witnesses of the arrival of the bodies at Laterina makes any mention of the arrival of an officer 'in an open staff car soon after the lorries'. There is nothing in the contemporary very detailed war crimes investigation evidence that points to the presence or arrival of another German officer unconnected with the Camp at the time in question. There is no suggestion either in the detailed list of suspects created by the war crimes investigation or in recent claims, that Lt. Waldheim was a member of the Camp Staff.

It is considered therefore that the evidence does not support any involvement of Lt. Waldheim with the Laterina Camp in Italy.

Other cases

In all the other cases of 'commandos' and 'non-commandos' which have been reviewed here there is no evidence to show Lt. Waldheim as having had personal responsibility for the interrogation or disposal of prisoners of war. There is no evidence that he personally participated in the interrogation of Allied prisoners of war or that he was present during interrogations. Further, there is no evidence that he was responsible either personally for, or for authorising, such ill-treatment of the 'commandos' or other individuals as has been established.

The presence of Kurt Waldheim's name on War Crimes Lists

The above summary of Lt. Waldheim's involvement contrasts with the presence of Kurt Waldheim's name on lists of persons sought on war crimes charges. The significance of such listings has not proved to be self evident.

Kurt Waldheim's listing as a United Nations War Crimes Suspect

The organisation and practice of United Nations' war crimes investigations had their origins in the joint declaration in 1943 by the United Kingdom, the United States of America and the Soviet Union which stated their intention to bring to justice those responsible for the war crimes that had been, and were being committed by the enemy. As part of the Allied war crimes investigations, the majority of the Allied nations participated in the body known as the United Nations War Crimes Commission (UNWCC): the establishment of this body was announced in London in October 1942. In later discussions it was proposed the UNWCC should:

a. Investigate and record the evidence of war crimes, identifying where possible the individuals responsible.

b. Report to the Governments concerned cases in which it appeared that adequate evidence could be expected to be forthcoming (4).

These two activities were seen as essential preliminaries if just and orderly trials of war criminals were to be carried out. A clear distinction was however drawn between the preparatory investigatory work of the Commission and any formal investigations and subsequent trials.

Before an individual's name was added to the UNWCC's lists of those accused of being war criminals by one or more of its member states, the case against the individual was considered by the 'No 1 Committee'. In the words of the UNWCC itself, this committee:

> although termed a fact finding body, performed such functions only in the sense that it determined whether ex parte material submitted to the Commission by its member Governments was sufficient to disclose a prima facie case. Its functions did not go beyond the determination of a prima facie case and were therefore not judicial. It could consequently be compared in Anglo-American law to those of a Committing Magistrate or Grand Jury. From the beginning its decisions were based entirely upon information submitted by member Governments. Possessing no information in refutation to that submitted by the member Governments and having no facilities for securing evidence from the accused or from those representing the accused, the Committee had to rely entirely upon the good faith, accuracy, and diligence, of the various member Governments in presenting cases involving bona fide war crimes (5).

An enormous number of cases were brought before the Committee. Therefore the consideration of individual cases was often necessarily cursory. For example, during the meeting on 26 February 1948 when Kurt Waldheim's case was presented, the Committee had to consider eighty-five cases, and the next day a further eighty-five cases were considered. By the UNWCC's own admission cases were passed almost 'on the nod': no defence material was available or considered.

The UNWCC listing of Kurt Waldheim rested solely on material submitted by the Yugoslavian authorities (Annex 210). The inaccuracy of Cpl. Meyer's evidence contained therein has already been mentioned (cf. p. 18). Whatever the reasons for the Yugoslavian indictment of Lt. Waldheim, the Yugoslavs failed to seek the 'listing' of either Lt. Col. Warnstorff or of Maj. Hammer whose duties and responsibilities fitted more closely with those alleged to have ordered the crimes in question. Both men were known to the Yugoslav authorities from the testimony of other German prisoners in their hands.

The British war crimes investigative authorities did not seek to list Kurt Waldheim with the UNWCC nor did it submit any evidence against him.

Kurt Waldheim's inclusion on the Anglo-American CROWCASS War Criminal List

Towards the end of the war in Europe, the Anglo-American command in Europe—Supreme Headquarters Allied Expeditionary Forces (SHAEF)—considered that, if the location and apprehension of individuals sought as war criminals was to be effected, some form of central agency was necessary to co-ordinate information. As a result, an organisation known as the Central Registry of War Criminals and Security Suspects (CROWCASS) was established in Paris under SHAEF's control. Although its work initially came from American, British, and French military sources, by the end of 1945 it had regular contact with the war crimes investigative bodies of all members of the 'United Nations', usually through the appropriate national liaison team. Only the Soviet Union failed to participate effectively.

The functions of CROWCASS were to collate details of persons notified to it by the various Allied national war crimes investigative bodies as being suspected of war crimes, as witnesses to these, or as security suspects. (These last were those individuals believed to pose a threat to the Allied occupation by virtue of their pre-surrender positions or actions). These names were then placed in printed 'Lists' distributed widely to Allied prisoner of war holding bodies and other appropriate agencies to help in locating the individuals therein.

CROWCASS had no investigative role. It acted merely as a means of collating and disseminating information regarding names submitted by others. A CROWCASS listing was not a judgement: it neither sanctioned the accusation nor endorsed the claim, as no evidence had to be submitted. The presence of an individual on a UNWCC list however was sufficient to have them added to the CROWCASS list. The presence of Lt. Waldheim's name on the CROWCASS list was a result of his addition to the UNWCC list: the CROWCASS entry shows that the charges came from the Yugoslavian authorities (Annex 211).

Kurt Waldheim's supposed inclusion on an 'Allied Wanted List of Top Nazis'

During the war Allied military intelligence officers, in common with their opposite numbers in all armies, sought to build up a picture of the enemy's order of battle. As part of their work they recorded the names of individuals within enemy formations and headquarters wherever they could in order that any information obtained that included names might be more easily recognised as originating from a particular source. This also meant that individuals who were taken prisoner and who might have especially useful information could be more easily identified.

It is in this context that the document described in Parliament by the Minister for the Armed Forces in 1988 (Hansard. Commons 9 March 1988 Vol 129. Col 217) must be considered (Annex 212). As the result of a debrief of a German officer who fell into British hands in late 1944, a total of 238 mostly German individuals were identified in varying degrees of detail. They represented those with whom the officer had come into contact during his duties in Greece in 1944, notably in Salonika and later in Athens. This document is in fact a supplement to a more detailed account of the officer's activities which includes several references in the text to Lt. Col. Warnstorff and Maj. Hammer and one to Lt. Poliza. There was no reference to Lt. Waldheim: he was included only on the list of names known to the German officer (Annexes 213 and 214).

These two documents provided the Allies with far clearer identifications of many of the Ic/AO staff at Army Group E Headquarters than they had had until then. But the Allied counter-intelligence officers, who were responsible for following up the search for individuals who were identified as being of interest to them, considered only Lt. Col. Warnstorff and Maj. Hammer to be worthy of registration in the index of those of counter-intelligence interest. Neither Lt. Poliza nor Lt. Waldheim was included in this register (Annex 215).

Neither this document (nor its companion) is in any way either a list of 'Top Nazis' or an 'Allied Wanted List'. Thus the presence of Lt. Waldheim's name in one of these two documents, as in the UNWCC and CROWCASS lists, does not challenge the validity of the conclusions concerning his limited personal involvement in the cases concerning British servicemen.

Conclusion

No evidence has been found that Kurt Waldheim was ever recorded in British lists of enemy personnel 'wanted' for detention or interrogation, whether as an individual war criminal, as a witness to war crimes, or as someone of counter-intelligence interest, or as being among those who belonged to organisations in the automatic arrest categories—the SD, SS, Waffen SS, Gestapo etc.

On the question of Waldheim having been of assistance to British Intelligence, it has been the practice of successive Governments not to comment on speculation or allegations concerning Intelligence matters.

CHAPTER 11: References

(1) Austrian Commission.

(2) Nigel Clive: A Greek Experience. Michael Russell Salisbury. 1985.

(3) Richard Capell: Simonata. Macdonald London. 1946.

(4) History of the United Nations War Crimes Commission, HMSO, London. 1948.

(5) Ibid.

Chapter 12: Remarks on gaps in the records and other records matters

Introduction

There have been allegations that some of the records of relevance to this subject have been deliberately mutilated or destroyed. The associated implication, if not the direct accusation, is that this was done in order to protect Kurt Waldheim from accusations of complicity in war crimes. These allegations call for a statement on the fate of official records concerned and on the procedures under which official records have been destroyed or altered.

A. GERMAN RECORDS

Of great importance in this Review have been the surviving contemporary records of the German forces in the Balkan area. Although a considerable quantity of these still exist, they by no means represent a complete set. This is due to several factors. First, as has been noted earlier (cf. p. 27), in September 1944, shortly before the German withdrawal from Greece, the AO of Army Group E Headquarters Ic/AO Branch issued orders to the subordinate formations to destroy papers relating to the Allied Military Mission and 'commandos'. It is difficult to be categoric as to how systematically this order was applied but in Army Group E's Headquarters at least it appears to have been carried out. Second, a study of the surviving records shows that, in common with most armies, considerable numbers of papers were routinely destroyed once their immediate significance had passed. This routine action was almost certainly supplemented by further disposals of material at various stages of the German withdrawal from Greece (Annex 216).

A third factor is that many of the papers of the German Army, which had been returned as a matter of course during the war to the Army Archive at Potsdam, were destroyed either by the Germans themselves or in Allied bombing raids.

The surviving centrally held German Army papers were captured by the Allied forces and were first assembled at Frankfurt. They were then shipped to the United Kingdom where they were available only for four weeks before they were shipped on to Washington. There the papers were catalogued and were also examined by the team from the American war crimes investigation body which was looking for material on illegal actions as evidence for the post-war war crimes trials: this latter team remained at the American Army World War II Record Centre from 1945–49. Where particular documents were selected, they received special annotations in the American accounts of the proceedings of the Military Tribunals. In some cases the originals were removed for inclusion in the war crimes trials evidence and photocopies were substituted in the original files. Although efforts were made to return all originals, there are cases where this was not achieved.

The American authorities also instituted a programme of microfilming this material. Although great care was taken during this process, it is not surprising that, given the size of the undertaking, there are occasional instances where items seem not to have been filmed as a result of oversight, or where files that may have become disorganised in their initial move from Potsdam could not be completely re-constituted.

Further, before the papers could be filmed they were reviewed by the American Army to check that disclosure of their contents was in no way harmful to American or other Allied interests. Under this procedure a small number of the total of records were felt to require further consideration before they were declassified, filmed and returned to Germany. Among the criteria for withholding certain documents from microfilming were that they contained 'interrogations by the Germans of Allied personnel' and references to British, United States, or Allied clandestine or secret intelligence activities. The classification of such material as 'CONFIDENTIAL' was a means of retaining Service control over the papers.

Once the initial declassification and filming programme had been completed—a programme which saw some 19,000 cubic feet of records declassified out of a total of some 20,500 cubic feet reviewed—the remaining portion, those still carrying a security classification, were re-reviewed and most were declassified and filmed (1).

As examples of the initial retention of some material, the outline details of two items initially not released but later declassified and filmed are attached (Annex 217). One is the 'Alimnia file' discussed below and the other another file including material on Allied clandestine operations.

The 'Alimnia File'

Although few documents concerning Allied 'Commandos' or Military Mission personnel have survived from the Army Group E or F archives, one significant item is the 'Alimnia Mappe' or file that was compiled by the Ic/AO Branch of Army Group F and sent by F to the Army Archive at Potsdam. The original contents of this file are detailed in the covering letter which accompanied it to Potsdam in January 1945 along with other material also noted in the letter (Annex 218).

This file was among the documents captured by the Allies and taken to America. There has been some speculation that certain pages were extracted from the Alimnia file and deliberately not filmed by the Americans and that these may not have been replaced in the file before its restitution to Germany. One reason for this suggestion is a note still extant in the original file (now in the Federal German Military Archives in Freiburg) which states 'Do not film this sheet, interrogation reports removed because of security classification' (Annex 219).

The US National Archives Guide to German Records Microfilmed at Alexandria VA, No 52 pp 24–43, shows that the initial filming, covering those parts of the files of Army Group F which had been declassified, was carried out on Microcopy T311 rolls 187-197. The F Alimnia file, which carried the old German Potsdam Army Archive number of 65605, had at some stage become mixed with other items from the F papers and had to some extent lost its original independent identity.

The Americans divided the larger file, which included the Alimnia papers, into a declassified part for filming (reference 65605/2 which was filmed on roll 189) and the remainder of the file referenced 65605/1 which was not declassified and therefore not filmed at that time. This latter section of the file which included the Alimnia file was also sub-divided: the 'Alimnia Annex' (as the Americans called it) was given a sub-number 65605/1a and marked 'C' for confidential (in accordance with the criteria mentioned earlier) as it contained material on German interrogations of Allied personnel.

However, this restriction was eventually removed and the Alimnia file was filmed together with the rest of Part 65605/1, both now declassified: both parts appear on T311 Roll 285 (Annex 220).

The authorities in both the American and German archives believe that all the papers from this file that survived to be captured in 1945 are now in the German archives file (2). But, to clarify the question of whether the whole Alimnia Annex was filmed in America and whether some papers have been removed from the Annex and not returned to Germany, a comparison has been made of the film and the original file and of the contemporary letter listing the file's contents when sent to the German Army's Potsdam archive in early 1945 (Annex 221).

This comparison demonstrates that the 'Do not film' note dates from the extraction of the Alimnia Annex from the whole file before the initial microfilming in America and that all the enclosures noted as having been sent to Potsdam in January 1945 and retained there are indeed in the original file in Germany. The comparison of the original file against the American microfilm reveals that some 43 sheets were apparently not filmed at all by the Americans. The contents of these pages suggests operator error rather than deliberate exclusion of material as the papers detailing the German interrogations of the British Alimnia prisoners were filmed, while other more routine German correspondence was missed. The fact that some items were filmed twice—the later filming occurring after the filming of some of the non-Alimnia material which had become mixed into the larger file at that time—supports this interpretation.

The use of the Alimnia File by the British authorities

At the end of the war there was an arrangement by which Britain and the United States could each obtain copies of the captured enemy records held by the other. As has been discussed in Chapter 7, the copies of the signals from the Alimnia file that had been extracted by the Americans for use in the OKW trial were seen by the British War Crimes investigators but these were the only items from this file seen by them. No evidence has been found to suggest that, prior to the commencement of this Review, the British authorities ever asked for or received a copy of the Alimnia file whilst it was in American hands, a microfilm copy from America, or a photocopy of the file from the German archives.

This may be explained by the fact that, although there was a British liaison officer attached to the Washington archive of the German documents, the enormous volume of this material made the discovery of any less obvious items very difficult.

Any searches under the name of 'Tuckey' or any of the other missing men would not have struck any direct chord in the American archives' index of the captured papers.

The 'Warren Document'

There has been considerable comment about the 'masking' that has been carried out on the German document containing the information gained by the Germans from their interrogation of the Cephalonia party of Allied servicemen and ex-German service deserters led by Capt. Warren (discussed in Chapter 6). This document was among the German Army records captured by the Allies and shipped to America in 1945. When in the years soon after the war, it was examined and found to contain details of individuals who had served in the Allied Military Mission in Greece, it was accorded the required 'confidential' classification. In such cases it was also common practice to apply a brown adhesive tape to 'mask' names and identifying details. This explains the censored passages in the Warren document.

By a careful study of the original document (since returned to the Federal Republic of Germany and now held in the Military section of the Federal Archives at Freiburg) and with the help of the Freiburg authorities, it has proved possible to reconstruct almost all the text of the document and to see that the masked areas contain no references to Lt. Waldheim and have no bearing on the question of his involvement with this party. The document has already been discussed in the detailed consideration of the Cephalonia party in Chapter 6, and copies of the original and the reconstruction are included there (Annexes 60 and 61). However included here is a copy of another document drawn from the German Army papers that has been masked in a similar manner to the Warren document as a further example of the nature of the information this action was intended to protect (Annex 222).

B. BRITISH RECORDS

These records fall into two groups, the larger of which was originally in War Office hands, with the smaller group in Foreign Office custody.

Group 1. War Office Records

The War Office material consists of:

a. The contemporary Service records relating to the operations in which the men concerned were engaged, primarily consisting of 'War Diaries' and other operational reports including signals and headquarters papers.

b. The personal service records of the individuals concerned.

c. The papers of the British Military War Crimes Investigations administered by the War Office.

d. The papers of the Intelligence Division of the Control Commission Germany (British Element), passed to War Office custody from the Foreign Office in the 1950s.

e. The papers relating to British interception and decipherment of German signals traffic, commonly called 'ULTRA'.

Group 2. The Foreign and Commonwealth Office Papers

The Foreign Office material consists of:

a. The FO files on the case of Sub/Lt. Allan Tuckey.

b. Other papers on prisoner of war matters and policy.

Before considering these records in greater detail, it will be helpful to explain in outline the procedure for the administration of official records and the selection of material for preservation in the Public Record Office (PRO), in accordance with the requirements of the Public Records Acts of 1958 and 1967.

In general terms, once a file is no longer in current use it is closed and passed to the archive. Some five years after closure, it is reviewed by Ministry staff to see if it is likely to have a future administrative use or potential historical value. If this seems unlikely, the file may be destroyed.

The files that remain are re-reviewed after about another twenty years in order to decide which merit permanent preservation. Most of those that are selected are passed to the PRO and made publicly available, usually thirty years after their closure. The Public Records Acts, however, allow for certain records to be retained in Departments for administrative purposes or to remain closed in the PRO for periods in excess of the thirty-year term for sensitivity reasons. The files not selected for preservation are destroyed. It should be noted that prior to 1958 there was no comparable statutory provision relating to the preservation of files.

Status of records

The status of the records listed earlier in general terms is as follows:

Group 1. The records in category a. above have been transferred to the Public Record Office although some are subject to an extended closure period. Those in category b. are not available to the public since they are held in confidence as between the Crown and the individual concerned.

Some of the War Office war crimes records at c. have been available in the PRO for many years and more are being made available. Of the contemporary papers in this category relevant to this Review most survive. The only serious gap is the incompleteness of the 'Rhodes/Alimnia' file owing to the absence of Maj. Barkworth's initial report which, as has been explained in Chapter 7, was mislaid in transit at the end of 1948. Subsequent papers from Maj. Barkworth and other related material have survived, however, enabling the facts of the case and its investigation by the war crimes team to be established.

Those papers from d. that were first selected for further administrative use, and then for transfer to the Public Record Office following the Public Records Act of 1958, have largely been available in the PRO for many years but some are subject to an extended closure period.

Considerable quantities of the material mentioned in category e. are already available in the PRO and much of it has been analysed and discussed in the volumes of the published 'Official History of British Intelligence in the Second World War'. A careful study has been made both of the material already released and of that which has not been released to the PRO. The results of this are reflected in the discussions in the foregoing pages.

Group 2. The FCO material in category a. comprises the 1948 file created by the Foreign Office on the Tuckey case. This is the only one that has survived from the series covering the period 1947–50. Some of the material on the destroyed files can be reconstructed from the registers in the possession of the FCO and from the personal papers of the Tuckey family as well as from the War Office papers. The 1949 file, which contained seven inward pieces of correspondence, was destroyed some time before 1958 when there were no statutory provisions for the preservation of public records: on the basis of the other evidence it is likely to have contained only inconclusive reports from Germany. The 1947 file, which contained both correspondence from Germany and with Lt. Col. Tuckey, was 'destroyed under statute' probably between 1974 and 1976. It was the equivalent of a 'case file'; only the most significant of these are kept and the reviewer would not have expected from the contents of the file before him that the case would develop as it did. The 1948 file was substantial and was preserved. The 1950 file was 'destroyed under statute' probably in 1979: if the reviewer had looked back, it would have been clear that the 1949 file had already gone and there would have seemed little point in keeping the inconclusive end of an incomplete story. Almost certainly each of these files will have been considered by a different reviewer.

The examination of the papers concerning these files indicates that such material as has been destroyed was disposed of quite properly in accordance with departmental procedures. The survival of so much of the material in other files is a demonstration that there was at no time a policy of systematic or deliberate destruction of relevant material to protect any individual.

As mentioned earlier, the Public Records Acts allow for the extended closure of papers or their retention by Department subject to the Lord Chancellor's approval. There have been allegations that additional material relevant to the matters under review is contained in official files not yet released to the public domain. It has been the practice of successive administrations not to disclose the contents of records which are so withheld from public release but such of these records as might be relevant to this Review have been carefully examined and the result is reflected in this Report.

The information available in the United Kingdom to Her Majesty's Government on the military career of Kurt Waldheim

As a result of Allied wartime work in building up an index of the order of battle of the German Army's formations, headquarters and their staff, references did exist to an Oberleutnant with the surname Waldheim on one of the cards concerning Army Group E Headquarters compiled by the Allied intelligence authority. The significance of these references should not be exaggerated. The reference on the card to a 'Lt. Waldheim' consisted only of a surname and post within the Headquarters: it was only one of several entries on the card, the remainder relating to other individuals. More importantly, as the order of battle index was arranged by Formation/Headquarters and not by the names of individual officers, it was essential to know in which unit or headquarters an individual had served if an entry relating to him was to be easily found.

As already discussed (cf. p. 103), Lt. Waldheim's mention in the German prisoner's debrief had not been considered of sufficient importance to record him in the 'counter-intelligence' personality index.

At the end of the war, Lt. Waldheim did not fall into British hands. Therefore he was not interrogated by British authorities before his demobilization and no further information on him or his war record was added to the existing wartime references in British records already mentioned.

No records have been found to suggest that, in the course of British war crimes inquiries, British investigators listed or made references to Kurt Waldheim by name or title. Even when the Alimnia case was finally investigated in 1947–9, none of the material appears to have contained any references to him. This lack of any mention of him in the war crimes context is reflected in his absence from the British index of war crimes and of individuals suspected of perpetrating them.

Clearly the United Kingdom received copies both of the final UNWCC List (No. 48 of 1948) in which Kurt Waldheim appeared, and the last CROWCASS consolidated list which noted the UNWCC case against him. However, as he was neither a suspect in connection with crimes against British persons nor a detainee in British hands he was of no interest to the UK.

The UNWCC file on the case against him existed only in Yugoslavia and in the UNWCC archives deposited eventually in New York at the UN. With the end of British war crimes investigations, it appears that little if any further study was made of war crimes records, especially those concerning individuals listed by other countries which had themselves apparently decided against further enquiries.

To summarize, there were very few references in the Ministry of Defence archives to Lt. Kurt Waldheim. In common with those relating to the vast majority of other German ex-service personnel who had been recorded at some time, these were not cross-indexed. He was not included in the alphabetical name indices created during and at the end of the war of those individuals considered to be of significant counter-intelligence interest because of their wartime role. Further, there are no references to Kurt Waldheim in the Foreign Office's indexes for 1945–50.

Thus the respective Governments of the day were not aware of the details of Kurt Waldheim's war record at the time of his candidature for the post of Secretary-General of the United Nations in 1971 (and again in 1976). No doubts were raised at the time of his candidature by any country or individuals about his war record and therefore there had been no apparent need to check records for references to Kurt Waldheim's military service after he was wounded and left the Eastern Front in late 1941. It was not until 1986, when revelations about his later wartime service in the Balkans emerged during the Austrian Presidential elections, that attention was directed to those areas where references to him might have been found.

CHAPTER 12: References

(1) National Archives Conference on Captured German Records, edited by R. Wolfe, Ohio University Press, 1974 and correspondence MOD—R. Wolfe NARA, U.S.A.

(2) Correspondence/Discussions MOD—Bundesarchiv, FRG and NARA, U.S.A.

ABBREVIATIONS USED IN THIS REPORT

AMM	Allied Military Mission
AO	'Abwehr Offizier' (Counter-Intelligence Officer)
BAOR	British Army of the Rhine
BBC	British Broadcasting Corporation
BE	British Element
CCG	Control Commission Germany
CI	Counter-Intelligence
CIC	Civilian Internment Camp
CROWCASS	Central Registry of War Criminals and Security Suspects
CSDIC	Combined Services Detailed Interrogation Centre
Dulag	'Durchgangslager' (transit camp for prisoners or war)
FAK	'Frontaufklärungskommando' (Intelligence gathering Unit)
FAT	'Frontaufklärungstruppe' (Intelligence gathering sub-unit)
F.d.R.	'Fur die Richtigkeit' (certified correct)
F.d.R.A.	'F.d.R.der Abschrift' (certified true copy)
Fr.H.West.	'Fremde Heere West' (Foreign Armies West)
FO/FCO	Foreign Office/Foreign & Commonwealth Office
GCHQ	Government Communications Headqaurters
Gestapo	'Geheime Staatspolizei' (Secret State Police)
GFP	'Geheime Feldpolizei' (Secret Field Police)
GHQ	General Headquarters
g.kdos	'Geheime Kommandosache' (Secret Command Matter)
H.Gr.	'Heeresgruppe' (Army Group)
HMS	His Majesty's Ship
HMSO	His/Her Majesty's Stationery Office
HQ	Headquarters
Ia	Senior Operations Officer in HQ
I Boat	'Infanterie Boot' (Landing craft)
Ic	Senior Intelligence Officer in HQ
Ic L	Air Liaison Officer Ic Section
ICRC	International Commission of the Red Cross
IG	'Infanterie-Geschütz' (infantry artillery howitzer)
i.G.	'Im Generalstab' (General Staff Corps officer)
IMT	International Military Tribunal for War Crimes, Nuremberg
ISLD	Inter-Service Liaison Detachment
Kgf	'Kriegsgefangene(r)' (prisoner of war)
Kripo	'Kriminalpolizei' (Criminal police)
KTB	'Kriegstagebuch' (War Diary)

LIR	London Irish Rifles
LRDG	Long Range Desert Group
LS	Levant Schooner (in this context)
MEF	Middle East Forces
MGB	Motor Gun Boat
MI9	Military Intelligence Branch 9
ML	Motor Launch
MOD	Ministry of Defence
MTB	Motor Torpedo Boat
NCO	Non-Commissioned Officer
OB	'Oberbefehlshaber' (Commander-in-Chief)
OFLAG	'Offizierlager' (officers' prisoner of war camp)
OKH	'Oberkommando des Heeres' (Army High Command)
OKW	'Oberkommando der Wehrmacht' (Armed Forces High Command)
Op	Operation
OR	Other Rank
POW/PW	Prisoner of War
RA	Royal Artillery
RAF	Royal Air Force
PRO	Public Record Office
RAC	Royal Armoured Corps
RAMC	Royal Army Medical Corps
RN	Royal Navy
RNVR	Royal Naval Volunteer Reserve
RSHA	'Reichssicherheitshauptamt' (Reich Central Security HQ)
RSR	Raiding Support Regiment
SAS	Special Air Service
SASWCIT	Special Air Service War Crimes Investigation Team
SBS	Special Boat Section/Squadron/Service
SD	'Sicherheitsdienst' (Security Service of Nazi Party)
Sdf.	'Sonderführer' (Specialist serving with Military Forces)
SHAEF	Supreme Headquarters Allied Expeditionary Force
SIPO	'Sicherheitspolizei' (Security Police)
SOE	Special Operations Executive
SOM	Special Operations Mediterranean
SS	'Schutzstaffel' (para-military body of Nazi Party)
STALAG	'Standlager' (Prisoner of War camp for NCOs and ORs)
Uffz.	'Unteroffizier' (NCO)
UNRRA	United Nations Relief & Rehabilitation Agency

UNWCC	United Nations War Crimes Commission
USAAF	United States Army Air Force
V-Mann	'Vertrauensmann' (Intelligence agent)
VS	'Verschluss sache' (classified material)
WO	War Office
W.F.St.	Wehrmachtsführungsstab (Armed Forces Operations Staff)

CHRONOLOGY

DATE	GENERAL GERMAN EVENTS	ALLIED FORCES	WALDHEIM'S MOVEMENTS
18.10.1942	COMMANDO ORDER ISSUED BY HITLER		
4.10.1943			Re-joins Army Group E HQ as 03 in the Ic/AO Branch
18.10.1943		1st LEVITHA PARTY CAPTURED	
24.10.1943		2nd LEVITHA PARTY CAPTURED	
16.11.1943		LAST OF MAJOR ISLANDS IN AEGEAN RECENTLY CAPTURED BY ALLIES FALLS TO GERMAN COUNTER-ATTACK. SOME 3,000 BRITISH TROOPS CAPTURED	
17.11.1943		LEROS PARTY CAPTURED	
23.11.1943			GOES ON LEAVE TO AUSTRIA
25.12.1943			RETURNS FROM LEAVE
6.2.1944		1st FORCE 133 PARTY CAPTURED	
19 and 23.2.1944		COMMANDO RAIDS ON PISCOPI/PATRAS	
25.2.1944			GOES ON LEAVE
26.2.1944	HILTER AND OKW ISSUE REMINDER TO ARMY GROUP F ABOUT COMMANDO ORDER		
25.3.1944		CEPHALONIA PARTY CAPTURED	
7.4.1944		ALIMNIA PARTY CAPTURED	
16.4.1944			RETURNS FROM LEAVE

DATE	GENERAL GERMAN EVENTS	ALLIED FORCES	WALDHEIM'S MOVEMENTS
18.4.1944		2nd FORCE 133 PARTY CAPTURED	
7.5.1944		YANNINA PARTY CAPTURED	
1.7.1944		CALINO PARTY CAPTURED	
1.7.1944		FORCE 133 INDIVIDUAL CAPTURED	
8/12.7.1944		RSR/FORCE 133 PARTY CAPTURED	
22.7.1944		SBS PARTY CAPTURED ON CRETE	
15.8.1944			GOES ON LEAVE
22.8.1944		RSR PARTY CAPTURED	
26.8.1944		COMMANDO/RN PARTY CAPTURED SIRINA	
3.9.1944			RECALLED FROM LEAVE
10.9.1944		RSR INDIVIDUAL CAPTURED	
28.9.1944		INDIVIDUAL EVADER MURDERED IN ATHENS	
13.10.1944			ARMY GROUP E HQ AND WALDHEIM LEAVE SALONIKA FOR MITROVICA, YUGOSLAVIA
16.10.1944		FORCE 133 INDIVIDUAL CAPTURED, CRETE	
27.10.1944		FORCE 133 INDIVIDUAL ABOVE ARRIVES MITROVICA	

Notes on Annexes

The copies of documents included as annexes are contained on the eight fiche held in the wallet on the inside of the back cover of this Report. Explanatory notes, including references to these documents, are included on the fiche.

In order to obtain better copies of poor original documents two pages, 190 and 582, have been copied twice and both copies are included.

p.221; Translation of Annex 60, the handwritten 'W' at the end of the text above the signature block is believed to be that of the then Lt. Waldheim.

p.253; This sheet which has not been translated merely confirms the distribution of the previous signal.

p.459 is a contemporary US Army photocopy of a document, hence its poor quality; for better copies see pages 431 and 433.

Errata

Please note the following typographical errors in the annexes:

p.4; References: 53 and 57 should both be Freiburg RH19/VII/16D.

p.9; References 212 should read Hansard Commons Volume 129, 1988.

p.218; On the re-type of Annex 60, the handwritten 'W' mentioned at the end refers to the 'W' located at the end of the text above the signature block.

p.288; the sidelining indicating the translated part is missing from the bottom paragraph on the page.

p.729, 730 and 731; 'Freiberg' should read 'Freiburg'.

Printed in the United Kindom for Her Majesty's Stationery Office
Dd.290154 C30 10/89